# Wood Wisdom

## H Catherine Watling

www.capallbann.co.uk

# Wood Wisdom

©Copyright 2012 H Catherine Watling

ISBN 186163 281 9
ISBN 13 9781861632814

**ALL RIGHTS RESERVED**

H Catherine Watling has asserted her right under the Copyright Designs and Patents Act of 1988 to be identified as the author of this work
No part of this publication may be reproduced, stored in a retrieval system or transmitted in any form or by any means, electronic, mechanical, photocopying, scanning, recording or otherwise without the prior written permission of the author and the publisher.

Cover and internal illustrations by H Catherine Watling
Cover design by HR Print and Design Ltd  www.hrprintanddesign.co.uk

Published by:

Capall Bann Publishing
Auton Farm
Milverton
Somerset
TA4 1NE

# Contents

| | |
|---|---|
| Foreword | 5 |
| Introduction | 6 |
| Treading the Forest Path | 10 |
| Birch | 15 |
|     Birch Tale | 22 |
| Rowan | 27 |
|     Rowan Rite of House Protection | 33 |
| Alder | 37 |
|     Springtime Journey: the Four Elements | 44 |
| Willow | 47 |
|     Willow Wand | 53 |
| Ash | 55 |
|     The Dancing Tree | 61 |
|     Meditation on the Three Worlds | 62 |
| Hawthorn | 65 |
|     Beltane Dance | 71 |
|     Beltane Rite | 72 |
| Oak | 75 |
|     Spirit of the Wild | 86 |
| Holly | 91 |
|     Holly Protection Rite | 98 |
| Hazel | 101 |
|     Rite of Bardic Eloquence | 109 |
| Apple | 113 |
|     The Bard's Vision | 124 |
|     The Apple - Fun, Fantasy, and Folk Games | 125 |
|         Apple Bobbing | 125 |
|         Bob Apple | 126 |
|         Pass the Apple | 126 |
|         Fortune telling with Apples | 126 |
| Vine | 129 |
|     Hymn to Dionysus | 134 |
|     Autumn Equinox Rite | 135 |

| | |
|---|---|
| Ivy | 139 |
|     Travelling the Labyrinth | 144 |
| Reed | 151 |
|     The Homeless Spirits | 155 |
| Blackthorn | 161 |
|     Triads | 164 |
|     Winter Meditation | 165 |
| Elder | 169 |
|     Samhain Rite | 174 |
| Silver Fir | 179 |
|     Fools' Paradise | 185 |
| Gorse | 191 |
|     Spring Equinox Celebration | 195 |
| Heather | 199 |
|     Summer Solstice Rite | 203 |
| Aspen | 207 |
|     Inspiration | 210 |
|     The Whispering Tree | 211 |
| Yew | 213 |
|     Yew Journey | 219 |
| Beech | 223 |
|     Walking the Beech Wood Path | 228 |
| Mistletoe | 231 |
|     The Druid Apprentice and the Mistletoe | 238 |
|     Winter Solstice Celebration | 240 |
| Bibliography | 242 |
| Contacts and Organizations | 244 |

# Foreword

The book and card set 'Wood Wisdom' is designed as a companion to exploring the sacred forest, both in the physical world and the inner realm of imagination, vision and dream.

The rites and meditations given will guide you along the winding forest path as you develop a feel for working with trees, but I hope that above all they will act as a spark to ignite the fire of your own inspiration. Poetry and tale are included for the same reason. Symbols speak direct to the subconscious: the word pictures of poetry, the visible images of art and the weaving of a storyline. They open the door to another kind of reality from the one we usually experience, where you can interact with the spirits of the trees and learn first-hand from them.

Finding a tree or grove that you feel a rapport with, blending the physical with the spiritual, is ideal but not everyone has a garden or woodland close by, or the privacy to meditate or perform ritual outside in peace. It is important to remember that, whilst taking every opportunity to contact physical trees, working mainly on the inner planes can still bring the gifts of knowledge and transformation even when it is not possible to get out into nature.

Any established Tarot spread, such as the Celtic Cross, or one you yourself devise, can be used for the cards, but more complicated layouts sometimes distract from the core purpose and have the effect of earthing rather than inspiring. As deep, if not deeper, insight can be gained simply by sitting in quiet meditation on a question or problem and choosing a single card, or alternatively three, to represent past, present and future; cause, effect and possible solution; physical, emotional and spiritual aspects..........A card can also literally be entered in vision - the world of its images leading to further images and new awareness.

From root to branch, may the sap of knowledge flow.

# Introduction

After the ice sheets retreated at end of the last Ice Age trees flourished in the milder climate, soon covering most of the British Isles. They remained undisturbed until around 3000 BC, when the first Neolithic settlers began to clear land for primitive agriculture, though for another three millennia, spanning the Bronze Age and Celtic Iron Age, these areas of cultivation were still no more than 'islands' amidst dark, impenetrable forest - a place of mystery and danger, as well as the provider of the basics for survival. Timber was essential for house-frames and fuel, wild animals were hunted for food, especially during the lean winter months, while domesticated swine could root amongst acorns and beech mast on the forest floor. The forest was treated with respect for the gift of its timber, for the ferocious boar and wolf that inhabited its depths, and for the sanctity of the trees whose lifespan far exceeded that of a human. There was an aura of wonder amongst the ancient trees, and shamans with their heightened senses were able to communicate with the indwelling spirits or dryads.

But the situation was about to change for ever. With ground clearance accelerating throughout the Roman and Saxon periods, by the time of the Norman Conquest only a fraction of the original forest remained, much of it monopolised for the noble privilege of hunting.

The 15th and 16th centuries saw the further destruction of around one million acres of oak wood to provide timber for houses, shipbuilding and ironsmelting. Any sense of reverence had now almost vanished and trees were seen simply as a commodity to create wealth and power, a commodity without which Britain would never have won naval supremacy or an Empire that at one time dominated half the world.

During the 19th century the continued indiscriminate felling of trees for industrial use, and urban encroachment into unspoilt areas, meant that cover was again reduced until by 1920 only 5% of Britain was forested. Today, this percentage has risen to 10% due to the work of such bodies as the Woodland Trust, though ancient woods, ie. those which have survived from before 1600 AD and consist of native broadleaved trees, are sadly rare. There is also a re-awakening to the sanctity of the natural world as more people explore Paganism, blending spirituality with green awareness.

Though, like modern Pagans, the Celtic Druids regarded all of nature as imbued with spirit, it is generally accepted that certain species of tree were especially sacred. Each of these represents the initial letter of its name in Gaelic in an alphabet known as the Ogham after its mythological inventor, the god Oghma. Despite some claims that the Ogham script originated in the Bronze Age, the earliest examples more probably date to the second century AD. However, this is not to deny that Ogham might well have evolved as an oral system for generations prior to being engraved on wood or stone.

The script is written by combining a series of strokes scored above, below or across a line - the 'druim', formed by the corner where two faces of a pillar stone meet or by the sharp edge of a wooden stave. The inscription, usually a memorial or a dedication to honour a deity, can be written horizontally from left to right, or vertically from bottom to top.

Our main source of information on the Ogham tree alphabet is the fourteenth century Irish manuscript 'The Book of Ballymote', which details the system's bardic and magical applications. As well as its tree correspondence, each sign was associated with a number of other objects possessing the same initial letter, thus giving Bards and Druids a secret cipher for communication with other initiates and a complex web of symbolism and mnemonic devises for use in poetry. Ogham could also function as a sign language by using the fingers to form the strokes and either the nose-bone, foot or shin-bone as the druim.

'Wood Wisdom' is dedicated to the twenty trees of the original system, together with a further two: mistletoe and beech. The former because it is the druidic plant most highly valued: the supremely sacred All-Heal; the second due to its strong symbolic association with traditional knowledge. And, though different sources give various species, or other symbols such as the sea, for the set of five 'trees' that became part of the Ogham alphabet at a later date, the beech is common to all.

The order of trees for the first group of five, which again varies according to source, is taken from *'Auraicept na Eces'* (The Scholar's Primer), though this differs slightly from that found in Robert Graves' *'The White Goddess'*, where each tree is linked not only with a letter but a lunar month. Often mistakenly believed to date back to antiquity, the tree calendar is in fact Graves' own inspiration, based on an early Welsh poem the *'Cad Goddeu'* ('Battle of the Trees'), a work that provides invaluable evidence for the importance of sacred trees in the British/Brythonic tradition, just as the *'Book of Ballymote'* does for the Irish/Gaelic tradition.

The oldest known version, recorded in the thirteenth century *'Book of Taliesin'*, is credited to the legendary Bard, though the actual creator will never be known for sure. What is certain is that the poem pre-dates the manuscript in which it is found, perhaps by centuries, having originated as part of a rich oral lore that was finally committed to paper in the Medieval period. There are several translations, amongst them D W Nash's mid-Victorian one, Graves' source of reference, and an evocative one by the present day Celtic scholar John Matthews.

The *'Cad Goddeu'* could well be a cipher for the Ogham alphabet, used by druidic and bardic initiates, or a poetic retelling of the events of an actual historical battle. Robert Graves' theory in effect combines both possibilities: the employment of magic and tree lore in a battle that took place during the fourth century BC over the possession of the sacred centre around Avebury.

Ancient associations between trees, wisdom and the magical use of letters are revealed etymologically in several languages, with the Irish word for trees *'fid'* being linked to that for knowledge 'fios'. In Welsh *'gwydd'* is translated as 'trees' and 'gwyddon' as 'knowledgeable one', while the word Druid probably derives from a combination of the word for oak - *'daur'* in Irish, *'derw'* in Welsh - and that for wisdom.

Celtic Bards, who before the Roman conquest were part of the Druid caste, frequently used metaphors connected with wood-carving to describe the sacred art of poetry composition. The northern tradition also associated wood with literacy, for example the old German word *'writu'*, the source of our word 'write', is translated as 'I carve', reflecting the fact that runes were once inscribed on wooden staves. We still refer to the 'leaves' of a book, which may originate in a druidic practice that involved threading actual leaves onto a cord or twig so they formed a message, decipherable only by initiates.

In Medieval Ireland the status of certain trees was laid down by the Brehon Law - an ancient legal system administered by travelling judges - where species were divided into the categories of Chieftain, Common, Shrub or Bramble, according to nobility and the practical use of their timber. The fine, usually a sheep or cow, imposed for unlawful felling depended on the status of the tree, a relic of earlier days when sanctity pre-dominated over material value and death was the penalty for felling a Chieftain tree.

But it must be remembered that every tree is sacred, not only those with a rich mythological heritage. After all, mythology and spirit connection are never static but always in the making.

# Treading the Forest Path

Before performing any meditation or inner journeying it is important to ensure that you will not be disturbed and are relaxed in mind and body. Turn the phone off and, if inside, sit or lie comfortably away from bright light and distracting sounds. Outside, clearly things are more unpredictable and what to do in case of interruption is dealt with later.

To achieve a deeper experience, and to assist in earthing fully after your return, it helps to begin and end a journey at the same 'place' on the inner planes, using the same procedure each time. There are as many ways to do this as there are travellers and the following is just one of those many ways.........

You have reached the sacred forest and, though its domains are deep and unknown, you long to explore, to seek the wisdom of the trees. In front of you is a simple gate with a latch or bar, and beyond it a track threading its way between trunks and undergrowth.

You pause to look at the path ahead, then take several long, slow breaths, feeling the strength of the earth stablilizing you and the sun and air pouring their energy into you. When you feel ready, focus on the intention of your journey and step through the gate, always making sure that you close it after you, a sign that for the moment you have left the mundane world of worries and distractions behind.

As you follow the path, smelling the scents of the forest, listening to the call of the birds and the rustle of small animals amongst the undergrowth, make a mental note of any features you pass: a tree stump, a fallen log, a stream......... After a while turn down a narrower track, secure in the knowledge that you will be able to find your way back no matter how far you wander, and continue until your quest leads you to the species of tree whose wisdom you hope to share.

Approach it slowly and with reverence, alert to the voice of your intuition. Is the tree open, willing to be communicated with more deeply? Or do you pick up an atmosphere of doubt or fear? It may feel most natural to approach in silence, greeting the tree and asking its permission wordlessly, through emotion and your inner senses, or you may wish to speak aloud, combined with ritual gesture such as tracing the relevant Ogham symbol in the air in front of you.

Providing you receive a positive response, move forward and stand facing the tree, sit with your back against its trunk or lie at its foot. The next stage of the work can now begin: meditation, journeying, receiving knowledge.........

Finally, when your communication is over step back to separate yourself from the tree's energy field, and give thanks before retracing your way back to the gate. Again, make certain to close it securely and sit quietly for several minutes before opening your eyes. To complete the earthing process, have something light to eat and a hot drink.

If you should be disturbed or for some other reason need to return to ordinary reality without having the chance to retrace the whole path, take a couple of slow even breaths and simply visualize yourself shutting the gate behind you. Alternatively, focusing on the solid earth beneath your feet can help you to feel grounded if there is no time to use any other method.

Whether the forest is entered in the physical or the non-material world, any tree that you approach deserves respect: greeting, seeking permission, working in harmony, separating, and offering thanks. If meditating out in nature, you have only to be aware on all levels, open to any commun-ication, however subtle; if journeying, one way to begin is by building up an image of the physical tree you are working with as you focus on your intention.

Inner or outer, once the intention is clear the exploration can begin.

The gate is closed securely behind you. You are following the path that winds its way through the ancient forest, seeking wisdom from one of the trees that grow in its depths or beyond, on the open marshes and uplands..............

A slender tree with a pearl-white trunk stands framed
against the vulnerable January sky.


Birch, Beith, Bedwen,
silvery, youthful one,
tree of bright beginnings.
Protector, herald of spring,
I come in peace and in search of wisdom.
My greetings and blessings to you and all your kin.
Is it your wish to share your knowledge and energy with me?

# Birch

The silver birch (*betula pendula*) flourishes on dry, sandy or peaty soil and is easily identified at any season by its white flaky bark patterned with dark markings. Fast-growing and rarely living more than a hundred years, the birch is one of the first trees to sprout new leaves in late March, while the flowers appear in April or May. Male and female catkins occur on the same branch, the male yellow in colour and up to 5cm long; the female, which are shorter and green at first, turn brown and extend before shedding a mass of small windborne seeds in the autumn.

Birch symbolism figures in the Anglo-Saxon, Norse and Celtic traditions, with associations of purity, birth and newness, probably due to the fact that the leaves unfurl early, combined with the tree's relatively short life-span and white bark. For these reasons Robert Graves has placed it at the start of the year, December to January, in his tree calendar.

It is interesting to note that when seen from above the birch seed bears a marked resemblance to the vesica piscis symbol, with the seed held at the meeting point of large curved wings, over twice its size. Just as the vesica represents the meeting of worlds, this world and the Other, the birch stands at the junction of the old and new year, symbolizing birth - spirit taking root in matter - as does the seed, any seed, ripe with potential.

As ruler of the month leading up to the ancient Pagan feast of Imbolc (2nd February), Christianized as Candlemas, birch can be linked with the deity Brighid (later St Brighid, whose holy day occurs on 1st February), who embodies the qualities of both a maiden and a mother goddess: purity and awakening fertility. Because of its delicacy and symbolism, the birch is seen as a feminine tree, and has been given the poetic/magical name 'Lady of the Woods'.

In the majority of Indo-European languages the word for birch stems from '*bharg*', translated as bright or shining; for

15

example the Anglo-Saxon *'beorc'* - birch, also the name of a rune, has the above meaning. It is the same as the root of the goddess Brighid's name, showing her etymological connection with light and fire. Beorc (Elder Futhark 'berkana') is the rune of birth, fertility and growth, and when cast in a reading is indicative of success in new endeavours and positive development in all areas of life.

The *Old English Rune Poem* (c. 9th century) describes the tree as beautiful, with a profusion of leaves, while the *Old Icelandic Rune Poem* (c. 15th century, but derived from ancient oral lore) adds that it is small and youthful, followed by the descriptive gloss 'protector'.

In the Celtic tradition, D W Nash's translation of the *'Cad Goddeu'* tells us:

*'The birch, though very magnanimous,*
*Was late in arraying himself....'*[1]

(ie. preparing for the battle), a metaphor which seems to contradict nature, as the birch is anything but late in producing leaves. Robert Graves explains this by saying that the lines refer to birch twigs hardening late in the year, not to when the leaves unfurl.

Mythologically, the birch is mentioned in a passage from the 14th century Irish manuscript *'The Book of Ballymote'*, the main source of information on the Ogham alphabet:

*'This moreover is the the first thing that was written by Ogham: b was written, and to convey a warning to Lugh son of Ethliu it was written respecting his wife lest she be carried away from him into faeryland, to wit, seven bs in one switch of birch: Thy wife will be seven times carried away from thee into faeryland, or into another country unless birch guard her. On that account, moreover, b birch, takes precedence, for it is in birch that Ogham was first written.'*[2]

Not only does the passage describe innovation and new beginnings, but advocates using birch in a protective spell against enchantment, based on the concept that purity/

virginity confers power and is a natural protection against harm. The tree's link with purification is also shown in the annual beating of village bounds with bunches of birch twigs, still practised today, and in the use of birch to beat or sweep out the spirit of the old year to make way for the new. Sweeping round with a birch besom is a good way to purify any sacred circle, but especially at the Winter Solstice or Imbolc it can symbolically cleanse the home or ritual area from what is outworn.

For similar reasons, criminals were once flogged with a birch rod, supposedly to expel the evil in them, an idea reflected in the caning, or 'birching', of school boys.

In birch we find the dual concept of purity and fertility, as is the case with the goddess/saint Brighid, Birch was often used for Maypoles, which carry phallic symbolism as well as representing the World Tree: its roots deep in the Underworld, its trunk reaching through the Middleworld of mankind and its branches spanning the Celestial World of the gods. The icy purity of early spring transforms into the warm fertility of May, the virgin becomes the mother, resulting once more in the inception of what is fresh and full of untapped potential. The two should never be regarded as mutually exclusive and not only are they combined in the person of Brighid, but in the Virgin Mary, stemming from her origins as a goddess far more ancient than her biblical persona.

Another aspect of the birch is shown in the Irish tale the *'Tain Bo Cuailgne'* ('Cattle raid of Cuailgne'), when the Ulster hero Cuchulainn uses it strategically against Maev of Connacht's army:

When Maev set her sights on the Brown Bull of Cuailgne, a prize possession owned by Dara of Ulster, she sent the boldest fighters of her land in a raid to steal the animal. As she and her host set out, her spies reported that the Ulstermen were all struck down by a strange sickness - the curse laid upon them by Macha that at times of crisis they would be debilitated like a woman in childbirth for five days and four nights. Only Cuchulainn, the son of the god Lugh, was spared the curse and left to defend Ulster single-handed.

Standing on one leg, with one eye shut and using only one arm (the traditional Celtic cursing posture), he cut a birch sapling, which he bent into a hoop and carved with Ogham symbols describing its creation. As he worked, he put Maev's host under geis (taboo) not to ride past until the Oghams had been deciphered and one of their number had created an identical hoop. Because this proved impossible, Cuchulainn succeeded in delaying them for one night, the period that the geis was in force.

Under Irish Brehon Law, in its Medieval form, the birch is classified as a Common tree, showing that by this time the classification was based on material rather than spiritual value. Therefore, the glosses for the trees which are honoured as Chieftain describe their nobility only in terms of practical uses for their fruit and timber.

By contrast, in an ancient Irish poem attributed to the wildman/shaman Suibhne Geilt we find the reverent words:

'O birch, smooth and blessed,
thou melodious, proud one,
delightful each entwining branch
in the top of thy crown.'

The birch's links with shamanism are two-fold. Firstly, in his or her spirit-journey the shaman travels to other worlds: via the World Tree, often symbolized by the birch in northern latitudes. Secondly, the hallucinogenic amanita muscaria or fly-agaric toadstool, frequently found in birch woods, was ingested by shamans to obtain visions and possibly also taken by berserker warriors to bring 'supernatural' battle-fury.

With natural grace the birch both protects and purifies as it stands at the gateway of the waxing year, its presence felt in all the spring festivals: Imbolc - the first stirrings of life, the Vernal Equinox - the first planting, and Beltane - the celebration of fertility.

**Sources for Quotes:**
1. Nash, D W, *'Taliesin, or the Bards and Druids of Britain'*. Reprinted by Kessinger     Publishing.
2. Matthews, John - *'Taliesin: Shamanism and the Bardic Mysteries in Britain and Ireland'*. Original source: 'The Scholar's Primer - Calder, G. (ed.), John Grant, Edinburgh, 1917.
3. Matthews, John - *'Taliesin'*. Original source: O'Keeffe, J. G. (ed. and trans.) - *'Buile Suibne'*, D Nutt, 1913.

Frost,
sparkling silver.
White, white visitor
in timid sunlight.
Winter's washed clean
the scars of the past.
In a pure pale shift
of pearl silk bark,
virgin birch rises
from her snowdrop bed
and stretches into the future spring,
bare branches dreaming of green.

# Birch Tale

Spring had arrived in the woodland, with soft step and gentle breath. At the touch of her hand delicate green buds cautiously began to unfurl on the branches of the birch trees. One by one they woke from their winter sleep and stretched towards the sun.

Then one morning, so early that frost still lay on the ground, the silence was shattered by rough voices and the stamp of boots snapping twigs and crushing last autumn's leaves underfoot. Chain saws whirred into action as the gang of workmen advanced. Jagged teeth sank into slender silver bodies, which trembled and toppled. Falling trees collided with each other, crashing to the ground, their branches torn and broken.

The men did not hear the screaming.

By the time the sun had melted the frost it was over. Rubbing grimy hands on their jeans the gang looked around with satisfaction. A good morning's work, they agreed. Where a stately silver family had stood, the bodies of trees lay prone, surrounded by their shattered limbs, a crumbling of sawdust blending with the churned earth.

The men lit cigarettes and drank steaming tea from flasks before setting to work again, hacking the wood into logs. With a dull lifeless thud each one was thrown into a waiting truck. Later, the severed pieces were covered with a pall of tarpaulin and taken away, sold to a merchant supplier of fire-wood.

No one saw the tears falling.

Throughout the summer the wood dried out in the yard, as the roots that had bound living trunk to earth were torn up and the area levelled. Without its grove the empty space waited, bewildered by human action, scorched by the sun, wetted by rain, weeds springing up in defiance.

With the onset of autumn the logs in the yard were sawn smaller still and, together with other species of wood, piled in cattle-feed bags to be sold.......

One cold winter evening, as I was stacking logs beside the hearth a piece of pale bark came away in my hand. Delicate silver on the outside, warm russet on the inner, it seemed like a gift, a thing of wonder not to be parted with. So I put it on the mantlepiece amongst the vases and boxes and candles, and there it stayed, long after the birch log it had clothed was consumed by the flames.

At the new moon of January I removed the bark from its place, intending to find somewhere safer. I paused with it on my palm, suddenly distracted by its subtle beauty. And, as my eyes slipped out of focus, I noticed a tall slender woman beside me, her figure draped in a white gown, her skin and hair almost as pale as the birch bark I held. With each moment that passed she became clearer, until the room itself was filled with a rich woody scent.

'Are you angry that I have what is yours?' I asked.

'Not at all, it's my only earthly dwelling now that my body has been destroyed, you hold my link between worlds. Come, I will take you on a journey and show you.'

She took me by the hand. The fireplace, the room, were gone. We walked out beneath a trilithon arch, following a path that curved through dusky woodland.

A white stag darted between the trees, lost to sight in a blink, and shortly afterwards we entered a grove made up entirely of birches. Above us, the crescent moon sailed between winter branches. Below, the ground was silver-frosted like the colour of the tree trunks, and in the centre of the grove shimmering fish swam in endless circles around a clear pool.

I went to the pool and cupped my hands, scooping up a handful of water and one fish with it, a fish that transformed into a horseshoe, echoing the shape of the moon. Filled with wonder, I placed it back in the pool, where immediately it returned to its former shape.

When I looked up again the Birch Lady was nowhere in sight, though I thought I heard her laughter, like silver bells, and it seemed as if many eyes were watching me, many bright voices whispering all around. I got to my feet, bewildered.

The laughter gradually faded, replaced by a gentle sobbing. And from the trunk of a slender birch the lady reappeared, her eyes clouded.

'The earthly being of this tree was once mine, as your earthly body houses your spirit.'

She stooped and picked a snowdrop, handing it to me. 'They flower early here. You will know me by this.'

'It's a lovely gift, I only wish I had one to give you.' I tried to think quickly, but I was wearing no jewellery, I had nothing at all with me.

She smiled sadly. 'There is a gift you can give, a precious gift: to tell my story.'

'Is there more to tell?' I asked.

'Perhaps. But now you must return to your own world while I remain here.'

She crouched at the foot of the tree and raised her hands. With a rustle of wings, a rush of air past my face, a dove flew onto them, fading into oblivion as swiftly as it had appeared. But, as the lady drew her hands down again, I noticed the small winged seed cradled in the whiteness of her palms.

Without looking back, I began to make my way through the woodland which was suddenly darker, no longer crowned by the crescent moon. Alone, I crossed over the threshold of the trilithon, back to the familiar warmth of the fireside.

Winter passed, and spring. In the summer contractors set to work on the levelled grove, imprisoning the earth beneath tarmac, though still the rebellious weeds sprung up.

Again, winter crept in with rain and frost, and the ground beside the newly laid road turned hard as stone. Seed and bulb slept in darkness until Imbolc, when a cluster of shy snowdrops opened out to greet the waxing year.

As I passed them something else caught my eye. Directly in the centre stood a tiny sapling, leafless and anonymous. Patiently, silently waiting, surrounded by its white-hooded guardians. Thinking only of the coming spring, I stooped to pick one of the snowdrops. Then, as my hand brushed the sapling, a familiar silvery laughter rang through the air.........

Roots held fast in a crevice, fiery berries contrasting with grey rock, a lone tree grows in the windy uplands.


Rowan, Luis, Cerdinen,
fey enchantress,
guardian over live and dead.
Vision maker, dream weaver,
I come in peace and in search of wisdom.
My greetings and blessings to you and all your kin.
Is it your wish to share your knowledge and energy with me?

# Rowan

The rowan (sorbus aucuparia) is both beautiful and ethereal, but surprisingly hardy, with a strong root-system that enables it to survive on the thin rocky soil of mountainous regions and upland moors. This habitat has given it the popular name of 'mountain ash'; it is also sometimes known as the 'quicken'.

The bark is pale grey, and the narrow pointed leaves arranged symmetrically, usually with six or seven pairs per twig. In May the rowan produces delicate clusters of white five-petalled flowers with a fresh perfume. They are followed by scarlet berries, which begin to colour in June and are vivid red by August.

Though the Irish Brehon Law lists the rowan as a Common tree, it is important for its associations with witchcraft, vision and the spirit realm, possibly because a pentagram - the remains of the flower-head - can be found opposite the stalk on each berry. And in Celtic tradition, any tree producing red fruit was believed to have Otherworld connections, so symbolizing death and rebirth. Red, the colour of life-blood and vitality, is also the colour of that blood spilt through violence. White, too, is linked with the Otherworld and death - the white of winter snows after all vegetation has withered, the white of corpse flesh, of the bleached skeleton......... It is these two colours combined that distinguish supernatural animals, like the white coated, red eared hounds of the Underworld Lord Gwyn (or Arawn), from their mortal counterparts.

The connection between rowan and the theme of life and death is found in the Irish tale 'The Wooing of Findabair', part of the epic 'Tain Bo Cuailgne':

The hero Froech, whose mother is of the sidhe, the Otherworldly faery people, wishes to wed Findabair, daughter of Queen Maev and King Ailell of Connacht. Yet he refuses to assist Connacht's planned raid on Ulster to steal the Brown Bull of Cuailgne, a task required as part of the bride price for

Findabair's hand, making Ailell fear the youth will elope with her and humiliate her parents in the eyes of the world.

Seeking Froech's death, Ailell demands that he prove his reputation as a champion swimmer by swimming in the Pool of the Rock of the Rowan Tree. He is then asked to plunge into the pool for a second time to pluck a branch from the tree, whose berries are said to possess magical properties and to be able to nourish a man in place of nine meals. When he returns unharmed, Ailell asks that Froech swim out yet again to pluck another branch, an attempt which finally rouses the water dragon that guards the rock. Findabair leaps into the pool, risking her own life to bring her beloved a sword but, despite managing to kill the dragon, Froech himself is mortally wounded.

As his life slowly slips away, a host of faery women bear him to the Otherworld where he is restored to health. Later he returns, strong and unblemished, to win Findabair's hand.

Froech, partly of faery blood, has a natural association with the Otherworldly rowan he plucks, and though the rowan is not given as the direct cause of his revival, its berries reputedly have the power of healing the wounded and of prolonging life by a year - reflected in the tree's alternative name, the 'quicken', meaning 'to give life'. The nine meals which the berries from the rowan in the tale are said to replace may well represent three meals consumed over three days in the Otherworld: the period of the dark moon and of death before rebirth.

Another episode from the 'Tain Bo Cuailgne' tells how the warrior Cuchulainn is travelling to confront the Connacht enemy when he encounters three hags roasting dog meat on skewers of rowan wood. His initial refusal to share their meal causes the hags to accuse him of discourtesy, driving Cuchulainn accept for the sake of honour. But the moment he eats, his strength fails, as he is under geis (taboo) never to consume the flesh of his totem animal, the animal that won him his magical name of 'Cullan's Hound'; and the breaking of the taboo foreshadows his death in battle shortly afterwards.

Rowan features again in the Irish Fenian tale *The Faery Palace of the Quicken Trees*, in which Finn MacCumhaill and his shaman-warrior companions, the Fianna, are put under geis to attend a feast at the hall of Midac, son of Colga. They find the hall in the centre of a remote plain surrounded by rowan trees, and immediately they enter, the band are awestruck by the smokeless fire, the brightly painted walls and the luxurious couches covered with rugs and furs. But before long the fire begins to spew out dark fumes, the walls become nothing more than bare wood and the fur-draped couches vanish into thin air. Now, knowing they have been tricked by illusion, the Fianna attempt to leave, only to discover that they are unable to move.

By activating his gift of fore-sight, Finn realizes that Midac intends to attack the Fianna while they are trapped, to avenge his father who was slain in battle by Finn's grandson Oscar many years earlier. He also learns that the spell was set by the Three Kings of the Island of the Torrent, who are amongst Midac's allies.

Fortunately, certain of Finn's men, including Diarmuid O'Dyna, have remained on a hill nearby and, sensing something is wrong, come in search of their comrades. As he defends the ford which guards the approach to the 'faery palace', Diamuid slays Midac and the Three Kings of the Island of the Torrent, whom he beheads. He brings the severed heads to the hall, where he sprinkles the threshold with blood to gain entry. He then sprinkles the ground beneath the men who are trapped, breaking the spell and enabling them to put the remainder of their attackers to rout.

The pentagram, seen at the base of each rowan berry, is the prime symbol of magical protection - the reason why sprigs of rowan were once nailed over cottage doors to ward off lightning and malevolent witchcraft, or worn as a personal talisman against harm. Fixing rowan above the entrance to a stable or cow byre was also believed to protect the stock.

Linking its symbolism as a guardian and as a tree of the Otherworld, in Wales rowan was planted in graveyards, in place of the more usual yew, to guard the dead and to stop restless ghosts from wandering, while in ancient Ireland a rowan stake would be driven through the heart of a corpse if the spirit of the deceased was thought to be unquiet.

In a contrary practice, Druids kindled fires of rowan wood on the battlefield, not to lay ghosts but to summon the aid of spirits in the forthcoming fight. Another druidic practice involved lying on bulls' hides stretched over rowan wattles in order to commune with the Otherworld through shamanic trance.

'The ruby berries' referred to in *'The Chair of Taliesin'* are almost certainly the fruit of the rowan, preceded by other ingredients in the Cauldron of Inspiration, the initiatory elixir that was drunk by ancient British Bards:

*Whence is the deadly dew*
*That kills the wheat?*
*And the moisture of the bee,*
*And the paste which it stores up,*
*And its abundant provision,*
*And the colour of the golden herb,*
*And the proper form of silver,*
*And the ruby berries.......*

This sacred drink symbolized the contents of the goddess Ceridwen's cauldron, which the boy Gwion Bach was set to watch over but accidentally tasted, causing his transformation into Taliesin: Chief Bard and seer.

As rowan groves are found on several Baltic islands linked with oracular practices, and can often be seen in close proximity to stone circles, to step amongst the rowans was to enter a place where the veil between worlds was thin. Carrying a rod of rowan can also help open the senses, enabling a diviner to find metal underground.

In Robert Graves' tree calendar rowan is associated with the lunar month of January/February, spanning the festival of Imbolc. Therefore, like the birch, it is sacred to the goddess

Brighid, or St Brighid, whose saint's day falls on February 1st. According to Christian folklore, St Brighid was foster mother to Christ, giving her the role of protector, as the rowan protects, as well as sharing the goddess'/saint's gift for healing. All are linked by the theme of fire - Brighid's fire of home, smithcraft and inspiration; St Brighid's perpetual flame at her sanctuary of Kildare; and rowan, described in 'The Book of Ballymote' as 'Delight of the Eye, namely, Luisiu, flame'.

Life-giving, protecting and enchanting, the rowan is a tree of power, respected and worked with from ancient times to the present day.

**Sources for quotes:**
1. Nash, D W - *'Taliesin, or the Bards and Druids of Britain'*.

Dusk waits in the shadows,
from the valley mist rises
like spirit-smoke from a Druid's fire,
weaving between the circle stones,
casting its spell amongst rowan boughs.


Time holds its breath on the threshold,
inhaling future and past
in the ghost wind that blows
through the grasses that dance
on the edge of this world.


The gypsy and the wandering Bard,
crowned with wreaths of feather-frond leaves
and berries marked with the five-pointed star,
tread softly as they enter
where the faery kingdom meets with ours,
and imbibe the heady draught
of its magic with open heart.

# Rowan Rite of House Protection

Before beginning, you will need to collect a sprig of rowan, with leaves and berries if they are in season, or two bare winter twigs to bind together during the rite.

Approach the tree slowly and with reverence, and make your greeting either aloud or silently. Then, rest your hand at the point where you intend to cut the sprig, using your intuition to sense if the tree is willing to assist in your work. If you feel any uneasiness, give it your blessings and find another which is more appropriate; if all feels right, cut quickly and cleanly. Give thanks and place an offering at the foot of the tree, for example a little milk or nuts and seeds.

For the rite itself, you will need a white candle in a holder and a dish of water - rainwater or water from a natural spring. If you intend to use winter twigs, a length of red ribbon or wool will be needed to bind them together later. You could also include two more 'altar' candles, incense and any objects from the natural world that you feel drawn to.

Place the items on a small table, or simply on a cloth in the centre of the floor, and light the incense and altar candles, but not the individual white candle. Stand in front of your altar, facing east - the quarter of the rising sun, of hope and purity.

Pause for a moment, concentrating on your intent to cleanse and protect your home. Then light the candle and speak these words:

> *Pure flame,*
> *White flame,*
> *Bright flame,*

*Gentle Brighid,
I ask your blessing.*

*Fire of forge,
Fire of heart,
Fire of hearth,*

*Radiant Brighid,
I ask your blessing.*

*Light that transforms,
Light that inspires,
Light that heals,*

*Be kindled in my soul, my home.
With the blessing of Brighid
All lights are one.*

    Pick up the candle and walk clockwise around each room of the house, feeling the power of Brighid's protection. After you return to where you started, leave the candle there to burn out, ensuring that it cannot topple or ignite anything.
    As before, meditate on your ritual intent, and when you feel ready hold your hand over the dish of water, saying:

*In the name of Brighid, I bless and consecrate this water, symbol of healing and purification.*

(The goddess Brighid was invoked for healing, while numerous sacred wells with miraculous healing properties are named after St Brighid, who inherited the goddess' gifts).

    Again when you feel ready, hold your hand over the rowan sprig, or bind two twigs together in the form of a cross, as you say:

*Gentle Brighid, I ask your protection and blessing on this house and all who dwell in it. May this sprig - or cross - of rowan be a symbol of that protection.*

Pick up the rowan sprig - or cross - and dish of water, and walk clockwise round the house for a second time, using the rowan to lightly sprinkle each room as you go.
Finally, give thanks to Brighid and to the rowan spirit, and attach the sprig or cross above your front door.

A stand of trees lines the margin of a marshland pool, their winter branches scattered with cones and last year's catkins.


Alder, Fearn, Gwernen,
eternal promise of spring,
buds spiralling to re-birth.
Bridge that spans the elements,
I come in peace and in search of wisdom.
My greetings and blessings to you and all your kin.
Is it your wish to share your knowledge and energy with me?

# Alder

Found on marshy land or growing beside water, the common alder (Alnus glutinosa) has an oily sap that makes it ideally suited to its habitat. It is a smallish tree with dark grey or brown bark, marked by a web of delicate fissures, and shiny leaves which are rounded in shape. In spring it produces catkins - the male with purple scales and yellow flowers, the female, initially green. But it is at its most distinctive in winter, when dozens of miniature cones can be seen clinging to the bare branches long after shedding their seed.

Robert Graves' tree calendar allocates the alder to the month running from March to April, the time when the catkins first appear, though in the Ogham alphabet it is often placed as the third letter, a tradition which I have followed.

Alder is a tree associated with re-birth after bodily or initiatory death, the spiral setting of its buds symbolizing life's cyclical patterns. The catkins and cones, retained throughout the dead of winter until new ones appear, act as another reminder of the continuation of life.

The '*Cad Goddeu*' says:

> *The alder trees in the first line,*
> *They made the commencement,*

a metaphor that may be based on the tree's early flowering, in February or March, or, according to Graves, that refers to the alder's position in the first block of five Ogham letters.

The Irish Brehon Law categorizes alder amongst the seven Common trees, though in Welsh mythology it has royal connections and is associated with the god/king Bran the Blessed and his nephew Gwern - the Welsh for alder.

In the Medieval Welsh *Triads* we find mention of the:

> *Three frivolous causes of battle in the Isle of Britain.*
> *The first was the Battle of Goddeu, which was caused about a bitch, a roe-buck and a lapwing.'"*

These creatures were stolen from the Underworld by Amathaon ap Don, instigating conflict between his forces and those of Arawn, Lord of the Underworld. The most detailed description of the ensuing battle occurs in the *'Myvyrian Archaiology'*:

> 'And there was a man in that battle, who unless his name were known could not be overcome............And Gwydion ap Don (Amathaon's brother) *guessed the name of the man and sang the two Englyns following:*
>
> *Sure-footed is my steed, impelled by the spur;*
> *The high sprigs of alder are on thy shield;*
> *Bran are thou called, of the glittering branches.*
>
> *Sure-hoofed my steed in the day of battle:*
> *The high sprigs of alder are in thy hand:*
> *Bran thou art, by the branch thou bearest -*
> *Amathaon the Good has prevailed.'* [3]

Without entering into debate over whether the 'Battle of the Trees' was a physical battle, a bardic contest or an initiatory exercise, it is clear from the text that alder is Bran's totem plant, a link also found in the Welsh *'Mabinogion'* tale 'Branwen, Daughter of Llyr'.

The myth tells how the Irish king Matholwch comes to Britain to seek the hand of Bran's sister Branwen, who is then offered to him in marriage. But her half brother Evnissyen becomes angry at not having been consulted and insults Matholwch by mutilating his prize horses. The conflict appears to be resolved when Bran makes reparation, and Branwen accompanies her new husband to Ireland, where she gives birth to a son, Gwern. Yet even after several years have passed, Matholwch's clan still harbour resentment over the episode with the horses, eventually leading Matholwch to banish his queen to work in the royal kitchens.

By training a starling to speak, Branwen sends a message to Bran, telling him about her situation, and he musters a vast army to march on the Irish. When the enemy retreat across the River Llinon, destroying the bridge, Bran himself lies across the water with hurdles on his back so his men can cross over - a sign of his identification with the alder, which produces a water-resistant timber used to support bridges and for the foundations of buildings constructed on marshy ground.

After initial violence by Evnissyen, peace is declared and Gwern proclaimed king, but when the boy goes to his uncle for his blessing Evnissyen thrusts him into the fire - indicating a symbolic link between fire and alder. In the tale it is implied that the boy is burnt to death, and Evnissyen's behaviour appears insane. Yet things may not be quite as they seem. Far from murderous insanity, the episode may represent the distorted memory of a sacred ordeal (possibly a firewalk) in which contact with fire does not bring death but purification and spiritual immortality, perhaps as part of the rite of kingship. Alder - Gwern - does not burn well as firewood, hinting that the boy did not burn either but received initiatory re-birth after ritual 'death', symbolized by the alder's winter cones and the spiral growth of its buds.

The theme of re-birth/immortality continues with Bran, who is grievously wounded in the fighting that follows Evnissyen's action. The king of Britain asks that his men cut off his head - the seat of the soul in Celtic belief - and bury it at the White Mount in London, facing the Continent. On the way east Bran's seven followers spend seven years feasting in Harlech and a further eighty at Gwales in Penvro, though throughout this time the head remains uncorrupted and capable of speech. Only when a member of the company named Heilyn breaks the taboo on opening one of the doors to the feast hall does the Otherworldly enchantment end, and the head is finally taken to London to be buried.

In Welsh, Bran means raven: a bird of prophesy, death (with continued life in the Otherworld), and transformation (initiatory self-sacrifice and re-birth). Therefore, Bran is linked to resurrection both through his totem bird and his totem tree. Robert Graves suggests that the names of the two are related - Bran (sometimes mutated to Vran in the Welsh language, as in Bendigaid Vran - Bran the Blessed) and Fearn (with the 'f' pronounced as 'v'), the Irish for alder. Gwern shares this etymological association, and both characters are so strongly identified with the tree that perhaps Bran's nephew can be regarded as the earthly aspect of the alder god, Bran himself as the Otherworldly aspect.

After his physical death, Bran's spirit remained as a guardian of Britain, connected to this world by his sacred head, which lay buried at the White Mount until King Arthur removed it. Even today, the presence of his totem ravens at the Tower of London, sited on the ancient White Mount, is believed to protect the land from invasion. Embodying Bran's power, the alder, too, offers spiritual guardianship.

Alder bark can be used to produce a red dye and the flowers a green dye, while the twigs give a brown dye, symbolic of the elements fire, water and earth, a symbolism found in the alder myths with Gwern's initiation by fire, Bran's bridging of the River Llinon and his protective head resting in the earth. Air is represented by Bran's voice - which continued to entertain his companions even after his head was severed.

The alder month spans the Vernal Equinox, a time of equal day and night, of life and death in perfect balance, as the tree's symbolism shows that in the eternal circle of existence neither ultimately predominates.

**Sources for quotes:**
1. Nash, D W - *'Taliesin, or the Bards and Druids of Britain'*.
2. Morganwg, I (compiled by), Probert, W (trans) - *'The Triads of Britain'*.

3. Matthews, John - *'Taliesin'*. Original source - Jones, O, Wiliams E and Pughe, W O (ed) - *'The Myrvrian Archaiology of Wales'*, Thomas Gere, Denbigh, 1870.

I have been a seed,
sleeping in the hard winter earth.
I have been a shoot,
reaching into the clear spring air.
I have been a tree,
branches strong in the summer sun.
I have been a cone,
scattering my seed with the autumn rains.
I have been a leaf,
fallen, to merge with the earth.
I have been a seed,
sleeping...............

# Springtime Journey: the Four Elements

The following can be performed at any time, but is especially relevant at the Spring Equinox. Before beginning have ready a handful of seeds, for example sunflower, and four pots filled with earth.

After placing a sprig of alder on a table or cloth, along with candles and incense, sit quietly and enter the inner forest, as always beginning your journey at the gate to the path.

Beyond the forest, across a low-lying pasture, you come to an area of water-logged ground. There, by the side of a river you find a line of alder trees, fresh catkins just starting to appear on their branches.

Descend the steep bank to one of the alders and offer your usual greeting, then visualize a titanic man take shape from the tree. The man carries a branch of alder in one hand and in the other a round shield decorated with the motif of two alder sprigs. You recognize him as Bran and ask for his blessing and wisdom.

Focus your attention on the theme of balance, and on the inner qualities of the four elements, all of which can be associated with alder. You see the design on Bran's shield as similar in concept to the Norse Fire Wheel or Celtic Cross, ie. a circle encompassing a cross. This symbolizes Bran's aspects, and the state of balance that occurs at the Equinox, with the dark subconscious qualities of autumn/winter (water/earth) and the light spiritual qualities of spring/summer (air/fire) holding equal weight; alternatively, it can represent the inner focus of winter, the outer focus of summer.

When you feel the time is right, thank Bran, and return via the gate.

After you have resumed ordinary consciousness, plant the four pots of seeds, one for each direction of the wheel, with an aspiration, seed hope, for the waxing year. Conclude by thanking the spirits of the four elements and again offering your thanks to Bran for his guidance.

Branches bowed to meet the water, a willow dreams on the shore of a glassy lake.


Willow, Saille, Helygen,
silken-leaved cascade,
that veils the secret pool.
Pale daughter of the moon,
I come in peace and in search of wisdom.
My greetings and blessings to you and all your kin.
Is it your wish to share your knowledge and energy with me?

# Willow

The willow (*genus Salix*) has many varieties and hybrids, most preferring a watery habitat, though the goat or 'pussy' willow will grow in drier areas like hedgerows and at the edge of woodland. Along with the grey sallow, it also differs from other willows in that its leaves are oval rather than blade-shaped. All varieties produce catkins in early spring, the male and female on separate trees, with the female releasing white downy seeds around May or June.

Classed as a Common tree according to the Medieval Brehon Law, since prehistoric times willow has been a sustainable source of raw material for making everyday objects. Varieties suitable for basketry are harvested each year by pollarding - the removal of all growth so that only the trunk remains to sprout new shoots the following spring. The pliable branches can then be woven into items such as sheep hurdles, fences or furniture. Traditionally, the supporting spars of the Irish coracle are of willow; and the wood of the golden osier is used in the manufacture of cricket bats, giving it the colloquial name of 'cricket bat willow'.

Willow bark is a natural source of salicylic acid, the active ingredient in aspirin, which can lower fevers, cure rheumatism and relieve pain in general, while its ability to thin the blood, reducing the risk of stroke and thrombosis, reflects the willow's watery symbolism.

Because of its habitat, willow has come to be associated with the moon, ruler of the tides, and with the feminine. The moon's three visible phases - new, full and waning - and its dark phase, correspond to the qualities of growth, fruitfulness and decay, followed by death/rebirth - similar to the yearly solar/vegetation cycle. Willow is mainly linked with the waning and dark moon, sacred to goddesses who govern not only death but magic, and in Celtic belief water provides one of the gateways to their Underworld realm.

There is a close association between the willow and

witchcraft, with the witch's traditional broomstick or besom being made from birch twigs secured to an ash stake by willow bindings. Some sources state that the word 'witch', like the name of the modern craft of Wicca, is etymologically connected to the Anglo-Saxon verb 'weet' to 'know', denoting a wise-man or woman, others believe that 'witch' derives from an ancient word for willow, though all three may well share a common root.

The willow's link with death and the Underworld is indicated archaeologically by the flint arrowheads knapped to resemble willow leaves that have been found in Neolithic long barrows. The association with death continued into the Celtic Iron Age, when wicker cages filled with animal, and occasionally human, sacrifices were burnt at the full moon to propitiate the gods in times of crisis.

'*The Song of the Forest Trees*' warns, '*Burn not the willow, a tree sacred to poets*' , a bardic link that is shown in the Irish tale of King Maon. Desperate to hide the fact that he has the ears of a horse, the king orders that every man who cuts his hair be executed; only the son of a widow is spared, on condition that he swears not to repeat what he has seen.

When the youth finds his promise increasingly difficult to keep, he is advised by a Druid to share his knowledge with a willow tree. He then forgets the matter until a Bard fells the willow to make a new harp. As he performs before the king the harp sings out its secret, revealing the truth about Maon's ears to the entire company, so preventing future executions.

Though this tale has a positive ending, willow is frequently associated with sorrow. Tennyson's poem '*The Lady of Shalott*', inspired by a French folk-tale, contains many references to the tree, setting a scene of Otherworldliness as well as of isolation.

'*Willows whiten, aspens quiver,*'[2]

round the island where the lady is imprisoned by a curse that forbids her to have any contact with the world except through a mirror. Finally, she sees and falls in love with Sir Lancelot and leaves her tower, bringing about her own death,

> '..........*Down she came and found a boat*
> *Beneath a willow left afloat,*
> *And round about the prow she wrote*
> *The Lady of Shalott.*

> '..........*And as the boat head wound along*
> *The willowy hills and fields among,*
> *They heard her singing her last song,*
> *The Lady of Shalott."*

'Lying, robed in snowy white'" she lies in the boat floating down to Camelot, an image reminiscent of the swan, a bird sacred to the willow which shares its grace and connection with grief and longing. And, like the swan, the Lady of Shalott sings as she dies - her swan song.

The Irish tale *'The Children of Lir'* recounts how his two sons and two daughters are transformed into swans by their jealous stepmother Aoife and doomed to a life of wandering, dreaming of their lost home and father. Such transformations, found in mythology worldwide, can be a metaphor for death or initiation, when the soul, represented by the swan, enters another level of being.

In the past, a rejected lover would wear a wreath of willow leaves around his/her hat, a symbolism that occurs in Shakespeare's 'Othello', along with the association between the willow and death. After he accuses her of infidelity, and shortly before her murder at his hands, Othello's wife Desdemona says,

> *'My mother had a maid call'd Barbara:*
> *She was in love; and he she lov'd prov'd mad,*
> *And did forsake her: she had a song of 'willow';*
> *.......And she died singing it:......'*

She herself then sings the song,

*'The poor soul sat sighing by a sycamore tree.........*
*Sing all a green willow must be my garland.........*
*I call'd my love false love; but what said he then?*
*Sing willow, willow, willow;.............'* [3]

Yet the tree also offers healing, directly through the properties of salicin, or through supplication to the presiding goddess, saint or water spirit of a sacred well. If a rag is tied to the branch of a willow growing nearby, as the rag rots away the sickness is believed to diminish. And in Somerset, one of the principal areas for osier cultivation, there is an association between willow and fertility. During the local Wassailing ceremony held on 17th of January, an ashen faggot bound with willow is burnt and a toast drunk in cider each time one of the bindings breaks, symbolically releasing the Earth Mother's blessing and power of abundance on the year's apple harvest.

Death, actual or initiatory, is followed by rebirth in Celtic belief, just as a willow cutting that is placed in the earth will not die but put down roots, living again as a new tree.

**Sources for quotes:**
1. Graves, Robert - *'The White Goddess'*.
2. Tennyson, Alfred Lord - *'The Lady of Shalott'* from 'The Works of Alfred Tennyson', Kegan Paul, Trench, & Co, London, 1883.
3. Shakespeare, William - *'The Complete Works of Shakespeare'*, Odhams Press Ltd and Basil Blackwell, 1947.

The new moon is sailing,
the river is racing,
the spring tide is flowing,
the young shoots are showing,
the catkins are growing,
as the willow, she wakes.

The full moon rides the sky,
the river weaves and winds,
the golden corn stands high,
the forest fruits grow ripe,
each leaf is green with life,
as the willow, she smiles.

The waning moon is shrouded,
the dark tide's on the ebb,
the barren fields lie cold,
the summer birds have flown,
the branches all are bowed,
as the willow, she weeps.

# Willow Wand

The magical associations of the willow make it a suitable wood for creating a wand, and as its element of water protects and purifies, both on the material and spiritual levels, a circle cast with a willow wand demarks a safe and sacred space.

At the full moon psychic energies and those of water are at their strongest, the height of their activity, also potentially at their most unpredictable and difficult to control. During the waning phase of the moon, the energies begin to slow, to turn inward and increasingly towards the realm of trance, dream and visionary experience. Either phase can be chosen to cut your wand, according to how you feel.

Approach the tree with reverence and offer your personal greeting. It is vital to be sure that it is willing to sacrifice a branch before you continue, as you do not want to draw negativity into your circle when working with the wand. After letting the willow know your intention and gaining its blessing, cut cleanly and quickly, then give your thanks and leave an offering in return for the gift you have received.

With a sharp knife strip off the outer layers of bark until you reach the smooth white wood at the heart of the piece you have cut. Leave it to dry out in a warm place for a few days before decorating with appropriate colours and symbols, though the fresh simplicity of the wood left undecorated is equally beautiful and has great power.

The wand should be blessed and consecrated with all four elements and dedicated to the service of the gods, to be used only for positive motives. It is really an extension of your own arm and forefinger, a focus for your intent when circle casting or consecrating, for directing the power.

According to western magical tradition, the wand corresponds either to the element air or fire, and is a male symbol. In the case of a willow wand, this is balanced with the feminine nature of the wood from which it is made, attuning it to both male and female energies in perfect harmony.

Dark buds still tightly furled, an ash tree spreads its branches above a spring meadow:

Ash, Nuin, Onnen
Lofty tree that bears the keys,
unlocking the shaman's secret journey.
Companion, burning ever brightly,
I come in peace and in search of wisdom.
My greetings and blessings to you and all your kin.
Is it your wish to share your knowledge and energy with me?

# Ash

The ash (*Fraxinus excelsior*), a member of the olive family, is native to all parts of Europe, and can reach the height of 40m. It has green-grey bark, smooth at first but ridged in older trees, and fine-toothed leaflets that grow in pairs from a flexible stem. The flowers appear in April, both male and female sometimes occurring on the same tree, at other times on separate trees.

The ash does not burst into leaf until May, later than most species, and throughout the winter and early spring is easily identified by its dark rounded buds, symmetrically arranged in pairs. During October it produces large clusters of single-winged seeds known as samaras or keys, which can be carried on the wind for considerable distances.

In Norse mythology the ash symbolizes the world tree, Yggdrasil, the Axis Mundi that links the three realms of Underworld, Middleworld and Upperworld. According to ancient belief, Yggdrasil's first root lay deep in Nifl-heim, a dark misty realm with a perpetual spring named Hvergelmir bubbling at its centre - home to the dragon Nidhug which gnawed continuously at the tree's roots, assisted by a multitude of worms. A second root was anchored in Midgard, the realm of mankind, close to Mimir's well, the source of all wisdom, memory and prophecy; the third was found near the sacred life-giving Urdar fountain in Asgard, the kingdom of the gods.

From the brow of an eagle perched on Yggdrasil's topmost branch, high above Odin's hall, a falcon observed all that took place in the three worlds, while the squirrel Ratatosk (Branch-borer) scampered from one level to another, providing a link, a flowing, between them, often through his mischievous attempts to stir up trouble between the eagle and the Underworld dragon.

Yggdrasil's evergreen leaves nourished Odin's goat, provider of the sacred mead of the gods; and the honey-dew

that dropped from the horns of four stags which also grazed on the foliage filled all the earth's rivers with water. The tree was, therefore, seen as the ultimate source for sustaining life, though its own life relied on external powers and in turn had to be sustained by a daily sprinkling of water from the Urdar fountain, a task carried out by the Norns - the weavers of fate. This, and Nidhug's ceaseless attempts to destroy Yggdrasil, to bring about the fall of the gods, shows how the balance of life and death, light and dark all existed in the being of the mighty World Tree. Beneath it, the web of fate was woven by the Norns, and the gods themselves met each day to hold council.

Odin, deified ancestor and archetypal shaman, who possessed the ability to journey in all worlds, was closely associated with Yggdrasil. After he gained the gift of prophetic wisdom by taking a draft from Mimir's well, he cut one of the sacred boughs to create his spear Gungnir. Later, seeking mastery of the runes, he used Gungnir to impale himself upon the World Tree in order to win power through ordeal.

When his nine-day initiation was over, Odin carved the runes he had won on the shaft of Gungnir, which shares the magical symbolism of its parent tree, embodying its essence. The handle of the witches' besom, traditionally made of ash, plays a similar role to the god's spear. Whilst out of her body, as Odin was during the time he hung upon Yggdrasil, the witch rides the besom to the Sabbat, gaining occult experience and gifts not to be found in the world of ordinary consciousness. Like the Maypole, the besom is both a symbol of phallic power and a link between the realms, accessible only to initiates.

Ash derives its name from the Old Norse word 'aska', meaning man, and according to Norse creation myth, the first man was fashioned from an ash tree before being granted a human soul by Odin. His partner, Embla, originated as an elm.

Though Celtic myth does not mention a World Tree, its

symbolism can be used to connect the three worlds of Annwn, Abred and Gwynfid. Annwn, the Underworld, features in several 'Mabinogion' tales, and again in bardic poetry, while Abred and Gwynfid occur in 'Barddas', the collected works of Iolo Morganwg. This describes Abred as the sphere of struggle and evolution, Gwynfid as a spiritual state where the soul exists in harmony, and includes another realm, Ceugant, the province of divinity alone. With the exception of Annwn, these are unlikely to be survivals of Iron Age druidic doctrine, but the product of the eighteenth century revival movement. However, the ancient Celts, like other tribal peoples, would have held a shamanic belief in ascending levels of existence similar to Morganwg's concept.

The Irish Brehon Law classifies the ash as a Chieftain due to its:

*'supporting of a king's thigh,' (ie. for making thrones) 'and half furniture of his arms.'*

The use of ash wood for spear shafts would explain the description in D W Nash's translation of the *'Cad Goddeu':*

*Very wrathful the.......
Cruel and gloomy ash."*[2]

Another possible explanation is that the roots of nearby trees are said to be strangled by the ash, and its dense shade discourages grass from growing beneath it. Lines from an early Irish poem, dating to the twelfth century, echo those of Nash's translation in describing the ash as baneful, and the use of its timber in weaponry is also mentioned.

According to the *Metrical Dindsenchas*, or place name tales, five trees were regarded as especially sacred in ancient Ireland, including three ashes: the Tree of Dathi, the Tree of Usnach and the Tree of Tortu. The text mourns their fall, and though it is not certain exactly how or why they were felled, the trees held great symbolic value, both socially and spiritually. Their destruction could, therefore, refer to the triumph of Christianity over Paganism, or to the loss of land or tribal power (see under Oak for further detail).

In addition to the documentary accounts from Gaelic sources, material evidence of the tree's sanctity is found in the spirally-decorated ash wand discovered on the Druid isle of Ynys Mon (Anglesey) and dated to the first century AD.

In both Wales and Ireland coracle spars were often made of ash, an exceptionally tough and pliable timber, also thought to act as a charm against drowning. An ash descended from the sacred Tree of Creevna was still believed to have this power in the nineteenth century, and Irish emigrants would take fragments of its wood for protection on their journey to America. Links between the ash and water go back as far as classical Greece, where the tree was sacred to Poseidon, lord of the sea.

But ash is most valued as fire wood, and features in a traditional folk rhyme with several versions, including the following:

> Beechwood fires are bright and clear
> If the logs are kept a year;
> Chestnut's only good,
> they say,
> If for long 'tis laid away.
> But ash new or ash old
> Is fit for a queen with crown of gold.
>
> Birch and fir logs burn too fast
> Blaze up bright but do not last;
> It is by the Irish said
> Hawthorn bakes the sweetest bread;
> Elmwood burns like churchyard mould -
> Even the very flames are cold.
> But ash green or ash brown
> Is fit for a queen with golden crown.
> Poplar gives a bitter smoke

Fills your eyes and makes you choke;
Applewood will scent your room
With an incense like perfume;
Oaken logs if dry and old
Keep away the winter's cold.
But ash wet or ash dry
A king shall warm his slippers by.

Throughout Devon and Somerset, the Ashen Faggot, a large bundle of ash sticks bound together with bands of hazel or willow, often took the place of the more common Yule Log. It was ceremonially brought into the house on Christmas Eve, then left to burn over the twelve days of Christmas. The four or more bands securing the Faggot were watched closely, and each time one broke a toast was drunk in cider. This is still a part of some traditional celebrations, such as the Wassailing held on Old Twelfth Night, ie. 17th January, in various towns in Somerset, ensuring the ash's continued place in folk custom today.

**Sources for quotes:**
1. Commissioners for Publishing the Ancient Laws and Institutes of Ireland - *'Ancient Laws of Ireland, Vol IV'*.
2. Nash, D W - *'Taliesin, or the Bards and Druids of Britain'*.

## The Dancing Tree
(Dedicated to an ash that grows below the slopes of Glastonbury Tor)


A woodpecker's beak
beats out its rhythm: a shaman's drum
summoning,
drawing the eye to see
what it has never seen before:
The Dancing Tree.

Limbs poised like Shiva
dancing the world into being.
Boughs shaping clouds
into serpents and swans.
Every twig a taper to ignite
the stars at dusk.

Leaden, then light
through lean and leafy season
the life-sap rises
up an ashen pillar poised
alone against the changing sky.

At its foot a gnarled root throne
draped with ivy and white-flowering thorn.
Autumn's bunches of copper keys
rattle a dirge for the passing year.
Summer plays soft waves of green
on the humming air.

And deep beneath the oldest root
a tunnel winds its way to where
the senses can only dream
and hear the earth pulse in time
with the ever-dancing boughs.

# Meditation on the Three Worlds

The ash can be used as an aid to meditation on different levels of being, using the concept of a World Tree which reaches from the depths of the Underworld, through the Middleworld of mankind, to the celestial realm of the gods. The Underworld relates primarily to the ancestors, either of blood, land or tradition, to the past and the unconscious, including dreams. The Middleworld is both the physical world around us and its astral counterpart. In meditation it can be related to the present. Lastly, the Upperworld is the realm of spirit, the highest source of wisdom. It corresponds to the future.

The Dancing Tree of the poem is an earthly tree, which for me symbolizes the World Tree - 'as above, so below'. Such a tree enhances the power of meditation if you work in harmony with it, always with honour and respect, and ensuring that the tree accepts your presence. Or, an ash tree can be approached and worked with solely on the inner planes. Visualize the tree, then focus on roots - Underworld, trunk - Middleworld, or branches - Upperworld, exploring the relevant associations. At first it is best to meditate on only one of the three worlds during each session, perhaps concluding with a meditation in which all are linked.

The above involves contemplation on the personal relevance and/or symbolism of other realms, while a second method of working with them is to actually enter into that realm, experiencing it first hand. This is not something to be taken lightly. It can be incredibly powerful and have a far-reaching impact psychologically and spiritually, so should only be attempted if you have experience of inner work, or are with someone who has, and feel in a calm frame of mind. Even then, exploration should be done gradually, getting to know the terrain and building up a relationship with the beings of that realm before seeking the answer to any profound questions.

After each meditation or journey ensure that you give thanks, and that you are fully earthed once you have returned to ordinary consciousness.

In the gentle warmth of a May morning the hedgerows are white with blossom:

Hawthorn, Huathe, Draenen wen,
bearing the frothy flowers of Beltane,
heralding summer's arrival,
and the blood-red berries that bid it farewell,
I come in peace and in search of wisdom.
My greetings and blessings to you and all your kin.
Is it your wish to share your knowledge and energy with me?

# Hawthorn

The hawthorn (*Crataegus monogyna*) is found in hedgerows, woodland and thickets throughout Europe, forming a shrub or small tree of up to 12m that can reach a great age. It is distinguished by grey bark, long thorns and delicate lobed leaves with a ragged outline. Clusters of small white flowers that have a strong acrid scent come into bloom at any time from early May to June, changing from white to pale pink as the season advances. The month of its flowering gives the hawthorn one of its alternative names - may, while the name whitethorn derives from the pale colour of its bark as opposed to the darker blackthorn. Deep red berries, or haws, which contain a single seed, ripen in September and are known by the folk names of Pixie Pears, Cuckoo's Beads and Chucky Cheese.

The lore of the hawthorn is bound up with the Celtic feast of Beltane, May Day and May in general the gathering of flowering hawthorn its origins in the cult of the Roman goddess Flora, introduced into Britain by Belgic incomers around the end of the first century B.C..

Despite hawthorn being placed in the rank of Common trees according to Irish Brehon Law, felling a sacred thorn was believed to cause destitution or a death in the family. This stems from the tree's connection with the Otherworld and faery, and in Rudyard Kipling's novel *'Puck of Pook's Hill'*, Puck utters the magical incantation *'By Oak, and Ash and Thorn!'* before transporting the children back in time. Kipling also draws on the thorn's Beltane links in the fifth verse of 'A Tree Song':

> *Oh, do not tell the Priest our plight,*
> *Or he would call it a sin;*
> *But - we have been out in the woods all night,*
> *A-conjuring the Summer in!*

> *And we bring you news by word of mouth -*
> *Good news for cattle and corn -*
> *Now is the Sun come up from the South,*
> *With Oak, and Ash, and Thorn!* [1]

Solitary thorns found on hilltops or growing over wells were said to mark an entrance to the Otherworld, so that anyone who fell asleep under one, particularly on May Eve, risked being taken by the faeries. The link between wells and thorns continued into the Christian era, with St Patrick's thorn in County Wicklow acting as the focus for a May Day ceremony in which people circled the well before tearing rags off their clothes and hanging them on the branches. Tying cloths to thorn trees at sacred wells, not only in May, is still a common practice in many parts of the British Isles, usually in the hope of curing sickness.

For centuries May Day has been a time for the celebration of fertility, when young people gather hawthorn boughs at dawn, sometimes after spending the night together in the greenwood. There is a taboo on bringing the boughs indoors on any other day, though hawthorn often tends to flower later in the month. Before the calendar was changed in 1752, in effect losing 11 days, the tree was more likely to be in bloom on 1st May, our 12th, though ironically, as we depart further from nature, resulting in global warming, it is coming into bloom earlier, around the date of its associated festival.

According to folk custom, hawthorn and other seasonal flowers are woven into May garlands along with brightly coloured ribbons, to represent summer's abundance. These garlands adorn the phallic Maypole, feature in dances and processions and, after the late nineteenth century, are used for crowning the May King and Queen. Prior to this, they were not usually crowned with wreaths of flowers but instead followed a large garland in procession.

Most modern May Day celebrations crown only a May Queen, though from Medieval times until relatively recently she was accompanied by a May King, and those playing the roles were not children but young adults. This has a far greater resonance with the Pagan festival, which celebrated the union of the Flower Bride - the goddess of summer fertility - with the Lord of the Greenwood, solar deity or corn god.

Hawthorn is often considered unlucky, but the blackthorn's reputation is more sinister, and when the two were found together, hawthorn or whitethorn, with its link to chastity, was once believed to destroy the blackthorn.

Christian legend surrounds the Glastonbury Thorn, a variety of hawthorn which flowers around Christmas rather than in May. The original tree supposedly sprouted from Joseph of Arimathea's staff when he plunged it into the ground on Wearyall Hill after first setting foot on British soil. But, despite its holy pedigree, it was felled by the Puritans as part of their attempt to stamp out the orgiastic customs connected with May Day.

The Welsh *'Mabinogion'* tale of *'Kilhwch and Olwen'*, probably the oldest of the tales grouped together by Lady Charlotte Guest, revolves around the theme of hawthorn as a restrictive influence.

The story tells how Kilhwch's mother loses her mind while pregnant, and finds herself amongst a herd of pigs when she gives birth - hence Kilhwch's name 'pig run' or 'slender pig'. She dies not long after, making her husband Kilydd swear not to marry again until a two-headed hawthorn grows on her grave. Seven years pass before he notices that this has at last happened, at which time he takes another wife.

When Kilhwch refuses to marry his step-mother's daughter, she lays a geis (taboo) on him that he will have no one except Olwen, the daughter of Chief Giant Yspaddaden (Hawthorn). The very mention of her name makes Kilhwch fall in love with her, and Kilydd advises him to go to the court of his cousin King Arthur to seek his aid.

After a year of futile searching, Kilhwch, Arthur and their companions finally track Olwen down. A detailed description of her beauty is followed by the statement that:

*'four white trefoils* (clover) *sprung up wherever she trod. And therefore was she called Olwen.'*[2] Her special qualities identify Olwen as a goddess of summer fertility, like Creiddylad, daughter of Llud Silver Hand, who is also mentioned in the tale of Kilhwch: *'for her Gwythyr the son of Greidawl* (the name Greidawl derives from 'scorch', ie. summer) and *Gwynn the son of Nudd* (dark Lord of the Underworld and winter) *fight every first of May until the end of time.'*[2]

Olwen tells Kilhwch that she cannot accept his proposal without her father's consent, and that he will never give it because her marriage would mean Yspaddaden's own death. Just as the hawthorn of his name guards its beautiful flowers with sharp thorns so he guards his daughter, the spirit of renewal and fertility. The theme is reminiscent of the hedge of thorny briars that grows up around the castle in the fairytale of *'Sleeping Beauty'*. The goddess of summer/princess can only be released/woken by the hero who must penetrate the Hawthorn Giant's power/barrier of thorns.

Undeterred, Kilhwch visits Yspaddaden to put his request, and on the fourth day the giant lists 39 'anoethu' or tasks that must be performed in order to win Olwen - tasks that are seemingly impossible. Amongst them he demands that her suitor find the Mabon, the missing Son of Light, a similar figure to Kilhwch himself, the young and virile Summer King whose role it is to conquer the old Winter King - Yspaddaden.

The climax of the quest involves removing a comb and shears from between the ears of the deadly boar Twrch Trwyth, to untangle Yspaddaden's hair. These items and a razor (not originally asked for) are eventually won at a great price, before Twrch is driven into the sea and never seen again. Following their success, the heroes return to Yspaddaden's court where *'Kaw of North Britain came and shaved his beard, skin and flesh, clean off to the very bone from ear to ear.'*[2] The shaving saps his power, symbolically cutting back the hawthorn, so the thorns are no longer an obstruction. Goreu ap Custennin then seizes Yspaddaden by the hair, cuts off his head and displays it on a stake on the walls. Arthur's men take the fortress and Olwen becomes Kilhwch's wife.

Mythologically, at Beltane the young god triumphs in the boar hunt, at Samhain (Hallowe'en) he is killed, giving way to the barrenness of winter. Therefore, the conquest of Twrch, like the conquest of Yspaddaden, places the conclusion of the Kilhwch adventure at the start of May.

The hawthorn, regarded as otherworldly, and unlucky unless treated with respect, is also a tree of celebration and fertility. It is the tree of the Pagan festival of Beltane, yet the beliefs associated with it have survived two millennia of Christianity in the guise of seasonal folk custom.

**Sources for quotes:**
1. Kipling, Rudyard - *'Puck of Pook's Hill'*, Macmillan, London, 1927.
2. Guest, Lady Charlotte (trans.) - *'Mabinogion Legends'*, Llanerch, Felinfach, 1992.

## Beltane Dance

Hold the hawthorn garland high.
Step, step and step again,
to the throbbing drum-beat,
drum-beat,
welcoming the summer.


Plunge the Maypole in the earth.
Dance, dance and dance again.
Twine the ribbons white and red,
white and red,
joyously united.


See the Belfires blazing bright.
Leap, leap and leap again.
Wildly dare the sacred heat,
sacred heat,
praying for fertility.


Crown the fair Queen of the May.
Sing, sing and sing again.
Place the blossoms in her hand,
in her hand,
that she may bless the living land.

# Beltane Rite

Decorate your sacred space with bluebells, hawthorn boughs in blossom, and any other seasonal flowers. If performing the rite outside, light two small fires, if inside, place two lighted red candles at the centre of the room in substitute for the fires.

The meaning of the Gaelic word Beltane (Bealtaine/Bealtuinn) is 'good fire' or the fire of the solar god Beli, and since ancient times fires have been lit to welcome the start of summer - season of light and plenty. Traditionally, jumping over the fire, or passing between two fires, was thought to bring good health, luck, purification and fertility.

If you wish, cast a sacred circle and request the blessings of the elemental powers of each quarter before saying:

*The sun is strengthening,*
*the sap is rising,*
*bluebells carpet the forest glade.*
*The sharp, bare hawthorn of winter*
*is garlanded with may blossom*
*as the old lord*
*cedes to the young warrior.*
*Kilhwch lies with Olwen*
*and the land springs with white clover,*
*green leaves and flowers cover the earth.*

*Lady of the May, Lord of Light,*
*I celebrate your union and ask your blessings on the*
  *land*
*and all who share it.*
*It is time to turn outwards,*
*to rejoice and live in the world.*

Pause for meditation. Olwen, the May Queen, goddess of summer, must be liberated from her father the Hawthorn

Giant, who guards her like the thorns guard the delicate white blossoms. In what ways do you wish to be liberated as summer begins? In what areas do you wish for fertility/creativity?

Feel the power of the waxing year within yourself and in all of nature around you. Then step between the two Bel-fires focusing on health, strength and creative energy.

Pause again for meditation, then give thanks to the gods and to the powers of the elements before closing the rite. Always ensure that you have doused any fires thoroughly after working outside.

A spreading canopy of foliage, supported by a massive trunk, filters sunlight onto the acorn-littered earth.


Oak, Duir, Derwen,
ancient King of the Forest,
who attracts the lightning stroke.
Sacred one of the Druid grove,
I come in peace and in search of wisdom.
My greetings and blessings to you and all your kin.
Is it your wish to share your knowledge and energy with me?

# Oak

The most common varieties of oak in the British Isles are the English or Pedunculate Oak (*Quercus robur*), which prefers the heavy alkaline soil of the Midlands, and the Sessile or Durmast Oak (*Quercus petraea*), more often found on the thin acid soil of the north and west. Other varieties include the Red Oak, the Pin Oak, the Turkey Oak, the evergreen Holm Oak and the Kermes or Holly Oak.

Oak makes up a large part of ancient woodland and has been established in Britain since the end of the last Ice Age. English Oak can survive for over five hundred years, with some trees reputed to be over a thousand years old. Historic oaks include those at Moccas Park on the Welsh borders and the 'Major Oak' in Sherwood Forest, mentioned in the tales of Robin Hood. Two gnarled oaks near Glastonbury in Somerset, known as Gog and Magog, are thought to be amongst the oldest surviving examples in the country, and bear the names of legendary British giants, names that originally occur in the Bible (Ezekiel Ch38 and Revelation Ch20).

English Oak varies a great deal from one tree to another, some reaching 45m in height though most are under 20m. Often the branches extend outwards as much as upwards and have a knuckly appearance, caused by the main shoots dying or being eaten while surviving side shoots grow off at a sharp angle.

The leaves of the English Oak have between five and seven lobes, with two small u-shaped lobes pointing away from the leaf at its base and stalks that are less than 5mm long. The Sessile Oak can be identified by leaves that taper gradually down to a long stalk without the extra lobes. In both varieties, clusters of catkins appear in May or June, followed by acorns which are ripe by October.

There is a fundamental association between Druids and the oak, with the word 'Druid' probably deriving from the

Celtic word for oak (the Irish *'daur'* and Welsh *'derw'*) combined with the word for wisdom (see Introduction for further detail). In a passage from his *'Historia Naturalis XVI'*, concerning the gathering of mistletoe by the Druids, the Roman writer Pliny (AD 23 -79) says:

*'......they choose groves formed of oaks for the sake of the tree alone, and they never perform any of their rites except in the presence of a branch of it; so that it seems probable that the priests themselves may derive their name from the Greek word for that tree.'*

Strabo's writings mention Drunemeton (Dru = oak, Nemeton = sacred place), while *'Pharsalia III'* by Lucan (AD 39-65) contains a description of a grove near Massilia (Marseilles) where, according to local belief, no animal or bird would take shelter, where the trees shuddered even on a windless day, and where serpents coiled around oaks which appeared to burn but remained undamaged.

Besides worshipping in natural groves, the Celts built sacred wooden structures like the one at Navan Fort, County Armagh, with its concentric circles of oak posts, the outermost ring measuring 130ft (40m) in diameter. According to dendrochronology (tree-ring dating), the oaks were felled around 100 BC, at a time when the druidic caste was at the height of its power.

The Irish Brehon Law classifies the oak as a Chieftain and asks:

*'What gives it dignity?'* followed by the reply: *'Its acorns and its nobleness.'*[2]

Though spiritual value is not mentioned here, the oak's 'nobleness' is seen as important, making it worthy of royal honour. And from the earliest times well into recorded history, each chiefdom had a vast and ancient tree, often an oak, which acted as the focus for the tribe. Local kings would be crowned beneath it, the life and power of leader and tree being so closely intertwined that if an enemy succeeded in cutting down the tribal tree it was thought to signal the overthrow of the territory.

In the early Christian period many sacred trees fell victim to the zeal of missionary monks attempting to stamp out Paganism. Lines in the Metrical Dindsenchas (place name tales) describing the Oak of Mugna, one of the five sacred trees of ancient Ireland, conclude with the statement that it was destroyed by poets, an act that seems inexplicable unless the tree was felled by the Druids/Bards in preference to abandoning it for the monks to cut down. But it was not always the case that early Christians disrespected Pagan sacred trees, and St. Columba (who trained as a Druid before being converted to Christianity) is said to have gone to great lengths to preserve the grove in Derry - a name that derives from the Gaelic for oak wood. He burnt the settlement and the king's fortress, but constructed his oratory facing north/south rather than the usual east/west to avoid damaging the grove.

Mythological evidence of the oak's importance to the Celts is found in the Welsh *'Mabinogion'* tale *'Math son of Mathonwy'*, both in connection with the hero Llew and with his wife Blodeuwedd. Because Llew's mother Arianrhod swears he will never marry a mortal woman, an unworldly bride is created for him by Math and Gwydion, using the flowers of oak, broom and meadowsweet. But Blodeuwedd is discontent in her marriage and takes a lover, Goronwy, with whom she plots Llew's death.

After the fatal strike is made with an enchanted spear, Llew shape-shifts into the form of an eagle and takes flight. His foster-father Gwydion then spends many days searching for him, until finally he follows a sow to an oak tree that she is in the habit of feeding under. When Gwydion looks up, he notices an eagle perched on the topmost branch, rotten flesh falling from its body to the ground.

Convinced that the eagle is Llew, Gwydion sings the following englyn:

*Oak that grows between the two banks;*
*Darkened is the sky and hill!*
*Shall I not tell him by his wounds,*
*That this is Llew?*

*Oak that grows on upland ground,*
*Is it not wetted by the rain?*
*By nine score tempests?*
*Its bears in its branches Llew Llaw Gyffes!*

*Oak that grows beneath the steep;*
*Stately and majestic is its aspect!*
*Shall I not speak it?*
*That Llew will come to my lap?* [3]

    In this way he coaxes Llew down and, striking him with his wand, returns him to human form.
    The eagle, into which Llew was transformed, not only symbolizes his solar attributes (a Gaelic name for the eagle is Suil-na-Greine - Eye of the Sun) but his royalty, as the eagle, king of birds, is often associated with the oak and oak deities. In both Scotland and Wales it was believed that Druids - wise men of the oak - could shape-shift into the form of eagles, and according to Scottish tradition, at Beltane sixty Druids would undergo this transformation before assembling on an isle in Loch Lomond to make predictions for the following year.
    Though Llew is equated with the Irish Lugh, whose feast of Lughnasadh occurs on 1st August to commemorate his death as sacrificed corn god, the account of his life found in 'Math son of Mathonwy' associates his death and resurrection with the oak, the tree allocated to the period that includes the Summer Solstice in Robert Graves' calendar.
    Amongst early Teutonic peoples, oak fires were kindled at Midsummer, in the distant past almost certainly accompanied by a human sacrifice representing an oak god or spirit, symbol of the waxing year and of fertility. Mythologically, he dies at Midsummer, slain by his rival, ruler

of the waning half of the year when vegetation withers and the sun loses its strength. His rival, in turn, would be slain at the Winter Solstice, when the days again begin to lengthen - a theme found in the Arthurian tale of 'Sir Gawain and the Green Knight', who carries a holly club to symbolize his role as spirit/god of the waning year. The Midsummer fires, accompanied by the symbolic spirit of vegetation, clearly were not lit to celebrate the year's decline but to acknowledge its imminence, and with the purpose of encouraging fertility and the sun's strength until the harvest was gathered.

According to the Celtic ritual calendar, which was not primarily solar, fertility rites would have been performed at the feast of Beltane, the start of the Celtic summer. Again oak played a major role, with the sacred fires kindled inside an oak log by rotating a stick, also of oak wood, rapidly to and fro until the friction produced a spark. That these rites, like those of the Teutonic peoples, once involved human sacrifice is suggested by a Scottish folk custom that continued into the eighteenth century. After a man had been chosen by lot, the company mimicked throwing him into the flames of an oak fire, then spoke of him as if he were dead.

In nineteenth century Germany, peasants still laid the hearth with a large oak log on Midsummer's Day, setting it so that it would smoulder for a year before being consumed. The following Midsummer, the ashes from the previous year's log would be mixed with seed and scattered on the fields to bring luck and encourage fertility. Customs surrounding the Yule log were similar. It was considered essential to keep it burning throughout the darkest night of the year or misfortune would befall the household. A piece of the charred timber was then preserved to kindle the following year's log, and in the belief that it offered protection against fire and lightning.

Acorns were also thought to bring protection, luck and fertility, probably because of the phallic appearance of an acorn in its cup. Carved acorns are often found as finials on top of gate and stair posts, and as cord-pulls. Though they are now simply used for decoration, it was once believed that an acorn at the door or hung at a window acted as a magical charm.

The ancient Celtic, Greek and Roman religions all associated the oak with deities of sky, rain and thunder, as it is reputed to attract lightning more than any other tree. The stricken oak brings the power of the heavens down to earth, linking the realm of the gods with that of mankind, symbolizing the flash of divine inspiration. And, in its role as World Tree, oak connects Upperworld, Middleworld and Underworld, its roots extending as far beneath the ground as its crown reaches towards the sky.

Poetically, the *'Cad Goddeu'* continues the thunder symbolism in the lines:

*'The oak-tree swiftly moving,
Before him tremble heaven and earth.'*[4]

The titanic Irish father god, the Dagda, presided over the oak, as did the Gaulish Taranis, lord of thunder, the wheel and the eagle. Other oak and thunder deities include the Norse Thor (Germanic Donar), the Greek Zeus and the Roman Jupiter, who had the eagle as his totem bird. Zeus' temple at Dodona stood beside an oracular oak, and on Mount Lyceus in Arcadia his priest would perform a spell to attract rain by dipping a branch of oak in a sacred spring. In Rome, not only was oak the tree of Jupiter, but the eternal fire dedicated to the goddess Vesta, and tended by her vestal virgins, was of oak wood.

The Celtic deity Brighid also had links with both oak and fire. Ruler of the fires of hearth and forge, and the symbolic fire of inspiration, she was daughter to the chief god, the Dagda - an oak deity. After Christianization she merged with St Brighid, who was born in the fifth century, the daughter of the Druid Dubhtach. The mortal Brighid did not entirely abandon her roots, and founded a Christian religious community at Kildare 'Church of the Oaks' (from *Cille* = holy place, *daire* = oak) where, as at Vesta's temple near Rome, a perpetual flame burned, tended by nuns. Even the Virgin Mary became linked with the oak, under the title 'Our Lady of the Oaks', in an attempt to Christianize the ancient groves.

Because of its connection with Druidry and magic, the oak, along with the ash and thorn, had an uncanny reputation amongst country people, shown in the New Forest rhyme:

*'Turn your cloaks,*
*For Faery folks*
*Are in old oaks.'*[5]

The first line refers to a belief that wearing your cloak inside out was a safeguard against being lured into the Otherworld.

Generally oak was seen as a hub of stability and security, and an ancient tree often served as a communal meeting place at the centre of a village. Many counties once had trees known by the title of 'Gospel Oak' where Christian preachers, following in the footsteps of their Druid ancestors, would disseminate spiritual knowledge. Beneath the famous Gospel Oak, which still stands in Highgate, Edward the Confessor renewed the City of London's charter by swearing an oath on the Gospels, an act that also re-enforced the link between the oak and royalty.

As late as the seventeenth century, this persisted in the tale of how King Charles II hid amongst the branches of an oak at Boscobel whilst fleeing from the Roundheads. After the restored king made his triumphant entry into London on May 29th 1660, the event came to be celebrated annually as Oak Apple Day, though it is possible that an oak festival existed around this date long before King Charles was associated with it.

Folk festivities for Oak Apple Day were often similar to those for May Day, accompanied by the decorating of churches and houses with oak boughs and the wearing of oak sprigs - not doing so meant being pelted with eggs or thrashed with nettles. More formal ceremonies, which have continued into modern times, include Founder's Day at the Royal Military

Hospital Chelsea, founded by Charles II, when oak sprigs are worn by all participants, including visiting royalty; the decoration of Worcester Guildhall Gates with oak; and a procession through the streets of Northampton, led by the Mayor and with citizens carrying bunches of oak apples and gilded oak leaves.

Alongside its sacred links, throughout history and prehistory the oak has played an important role in the daily life of humankind, providing strong timber for the construction of houses, furniture and sailing craft. A reminder of this legacy still exists in our word 'door', which derives from the Gaelic and Sanskrit for oak - *duir*.

**Sources for quotes:**
1. Kendrick, T D - *'Druids or a Study in Celtic Prehistory'*.
2. Commissioners for Publishing the Ancient Laws and Institutes of Ireland - *'Ancient Laws of Ireland, Vol IV'*.
3. Guest, Lady Charlotte (trans) - *'Mabinogion - The Four Branches'*.
4. Nash, D W - *'Taliesin, or the Bards and Druids of Britain'*.
5. Valiente, Doreen - *'An ABC of Witchcraft, Past and Present'*, Robert Hale, London, 1986.

Acorns fall from the branch
of their parent tree,
to rest on a leafy bed
under a canopy of
holly, oak and beech
that reaches as far as the eye can see.

One sapling with leaves that seem
too large for its slender stem,
spared by squirrel and hungry deer,
feels the sunlight of its first spring
and gentle rain through a canopy
that reaches as far as the eye can see.

A youthful, straight-trunked tree,
encircled by the elder oaks,
puts forth late summer shoots
as man and swine amble by
and forage under the canopy
that reaches as far as the eye can see.

Fifty rings to mark the years,
clustered acorns on its boughs,
the tree stands tall as mighty
ancestors fall to man's axe blows,
and gaps appear in the canopy
that reaches as far as the eye can see.

Around its proud oak father
each year the forest springs anew,
now slashed in two by a stony path
that takes both horse and wagon
to the end of the canopy and fields
that reach as far as the eye can see.

Gnarled and knuckled, ancient tree,
who would be greenwood king,
holds court alone beside the road
where cars rush past a single canopy
to a forest of glass and concrete
that reaches as far as the eye can see.

# Spirit of the Wild

'Sean!' the village blacksmith yelled out as a fair-haired youth strolled past the forge on his way back from afternoon milking. 'Will you run an errand for me?'

Sean turned to look at the familiar broad face smeared with sweat and smoke from the furnace, at the heavily muscled arms above the leather apron, as always feeling a sense of awe. Not only did he have great physical strength, but there was an aura of magic, of the Otherworld, about the smith. It was a privilege to have been chosen to help him.

'What is it you want me to do?'

'Old Reilly over at Winterford was expecting these shears at noon. They weren't done when he called.........' Putting aside the ploughshare he was working on, the smith handed them across. 'Remember the blades are sharp, boy, and don't dawdle, I'm putting my trust in you.'

With his burden tucked under his arm, Sean continued on his way. The most direct route to the next village was through the forest, though most people took the open path that curved between the river and the cattle pasture, afraid of getting lost amongst the dark trees or of the dryad spirits said to dwell in them. Sean had taken the forest path several times with his older brothers, but now he was almost a man and could face it alone. He wanted to prove it to himself, besides, the less time he took getting to Winterford the more he would have to sit at Jim Reilly's hearth and hear the wild tales of when he was young. It was a crisp early autumn day with the leaves just beginning to turn and the sky a distant blue. There seemed nothing uncanny about the forest as Sean set out at an even pace, making certain not to stray from the path which was barely visible between swathes of ivy and bramble. Occasionally a bird trilled out its autumn call, a more wistful note than the songs of spring and high summer, or a small animal moved unseen amongst the ground cover, otherwise all was still.

At first Sean felt relaxed, at home even, surrounded by peace and beauty, then slowly, very slowly, he became aware of a new sense - the sense of being an outsider, like the stranger who sits by the hearthfire, noticing the wary silences and suspicious looks of the villagers. He had always thought of the oaks in the forest as majestic, yet somehow only there by the will of his people and for their benefit. At any time the mightiest tree could be felled to provide a new roof beam Now he had a feeling that the position was reversed - he was in their territory, at their mercy. Though, instead of running in fear, he began to walk more slowly. If he missed the path they would truly prove their superiority over him.

Never before had he questioned his own identity, but the trees seemed to mock his short lifespan, his movements, his racing thoughts. Everything about them was a world away from his experience - not seeing, not hearing, living always in one space, never laughing nor crying, yet alive. And aware of him, he was certain. He could feel the weight of the alienation bearing down on him, so the trees' massive static presence seemed suffocating - their great gnarled roots twining deep into the earth were entangling themselves in his mind. He reminded himself that they held no malice, not as men did, but even such a thought was disquieting. No anger, no love, except that the leaves loved the air and sun, the roots loved the rain and the earth. Once, in the hope of reaching some understanding, he stopped beside one of the oaks, only to find a gulf between them that he had no idea how to cross.

With a kind of relief he watched a squirrel shin up a cracked trunk, animals at least moved and ate as men did. Then the gulf yawned wider still. Bird, squirrel, ivy and oak were all part of the spirit of the forest. Different though they were from each other, they were not human, their lives were woven together in harmony while he continued to plod clumsily along the path. What bird or animal feared to lose its way or needed to build a fire for survival. In the multi-coloured tapestry of the woodland he was the loose thread, unable to blend in.

As the sense of alienation increased it degenerated into fear. He was in the deepest part of the forest now, where the oak canopy was so dense overhead he could scarcely see the sky, and it had become darker, the sun was no longer shimmering on the leaves in a dance of gold. Nor could Sean make out the path any more - neither behind nor ahead of him. The bright red poisonous berries of Lords and Ladies lured like wreckers' lights amongst the undergrowth, and toadstools nestled at the foot of the trees. It crossed his mind that if he was lost and starving he could eat blackberries, most other things he was too wary of. But the birds and animals knew what was safe to eat. This was their world. A world humankind had separated itself from.

Every time a twig snapped or a leaf fell, flitting softly against the other leaves, he would jump and turn sharply. What if there were dangerous beasts here? Wild boars? Wolves?

Just as the thought came to him, Sean sensed that something larger than the usual squirrel or dormouse was moving stealthily through the bushes. If he had known which way to run, he would have run, but instead he froze. He felt certain that he could see a huge dark shape approaching, at the same moment the trees seemed to be moving closer, their tops leaning in towards him as brambles bound his ankles like barbed wire, then, as his head span with terror he found himself looking into a pair of calm hazel eyes. The fox's expression was puzzled, a little condescending. It paused for a moment, before continuing with an air of unhurried purpose.

Sean let out a long breath, relieved to find that the trees were no closer after all and that the track ahead had not entirely disappeared from view. Eventually, summoning his courage, he began to pick his way along it. And, as he walked, he glanced around to see if he could spot the fox again, remembering the look it had given him as clearly as if their gaze was still locked, eye to eye. Two travellers whose paths had crossed. What was its errand? To bring food for its young? To seek out fresh water? A sheltered place to sleep?

There was no sign of his fellow traveller, but Sean now viewed the trees with a new awareness. Though they were not there for man's convenience, they could live in harmony, blending and intermingling, if man managed the forests well, cutting branches, rather than felling whole trees, and protecting the young saplings. For millions of years the forests had nurtured man as they nurtured the fox and the squirrel. If Sean had been lost he could have found shelter in a hollow trunk or covered himself with a blanket of fallen leaves, like a hibernating animal. He could even have climbed up into the branches if he felt vulnerable on the ground. A living oak offered security, just as his family's oak-framed house did. His senses were untrained, reacting out of proportion to the situation, but the fear he had felt at the approach of the fox was akin to the fear of the dormouse. And yes, he could have eaten blackberries - or acorns, hazel or beech nuts. He was not so far removed from the forest and its gifts after all.

As unexpected thoughts filtered through, like sunlight through the forest canopy, for the first time he noticed jewel-like beetles on the rotten logs that blocked his path, saw intricate patterns in the deeply ridged bark of the oaks, was uplifted by a flash of colour on a bird's wing. Through sheer wonder he forgot himself and his fears, and did not realize how far he had walked until he caught a glimpse of a thatched roof between the trees up ahead. So Reilly's shears would be safely delivered, and soon he would be sitting by a warm fire, listening to the old man's tales. Though now he had a tale of his own to tell, and knew that for the rest of his life he would carry a part of the wild forest in his soul.

Amongst the dead foliage of winter, a bush with waxy green leaves and blood-red berries shines out like a beacon in the woodland:


Holly, Tinne, Celynnen,
noble warrior,
strong your shining armour.
Brave defender of truth,
I come in peace and in search of wisdom.
My greetings and blessings to you and all your kin.
Is it your wish to share your knowledge and energy with me?

# Holly

The holly (*Ilex aquifolium*) is an evergreen found either as a low shrub or as a pyramid-shaped tree of up to 20m in height. It is common in hedgerows and woodland throughout western Europe, and occurs in all areas of Britain except the far north. Its distinctive dark leaves have sharp spines lower down the trunk, though on the upper branches, above the reach of grazing animals, they are spineless.

In May the holly produces small white flowers, the male and female on separate trees. The berries, which begin to appear in July, are green at first but gradually ripen to red in September.

In the Irish Ogham alphabet holly is *'tinne'*, meaning fire, though in Welsh it is *'celynnen'*, instead of sharing the Welsh word for fire, *'tan'*. Robert Graves states that *'dann'* ('tann'), which equates with *'tinne'*, was the word used by the Celts to describe any sacred tree. In Gaul and Brittany it referred to the oak, in Cornwall *'glas-tann'* ('green sacred tree') meant evergreen holm-oak, but holly rather than evergreen oak played a major role in the Roman Midwinter feast of the Saturnalia. A chain of association which, if taken full circle, leads to the theory that an ancient Brythonic name for holly was in fact 'tan'.

Graves' tree calendar assigns holly to July, but it is more commonly linked with Midwinter, its evergreen leaves representing life at a time when most vegetation is dead and leafless. The scarlet berries carry the same meaning, or can evoke the blood of sacrifice. They also symbolize light, fire and warmth in the dark months.

For these reasons, holly has been brought inside during the festive season for centuries. Teutonic peoples blessed loved ones with health, strength and fertility by touching them with holly. And the Romans used it for decoration and as a gift at the Saturnalia, celebrated over seven days around the Winter Solstice in honour of Saturn - an ancient

agricultural deity, later identified with the Greek Kronos to become lord of time and old age - who ruled the waning year, wielding a club of holly.

Mythologically, the god of the waning year slays his rival, fertile deity of the waxing year, at the Summer Solstice, reigning until he in turn is slain at the Winter Solstice. This eternal battle between the god of summer, often represented by the oak, and the god of winter/ holly features in several tales, including *'Sir Gawain and the Green Knight'* - the latter with his holly club embodying Saturn's power. He enters King Arthur's hall at New Year, asking anyone who has the courage to step forward and strike him with the axe he carries, providing he can reciprocate in a year's time. Sir Gawain accepts the challenge, beheading, but not killing, the Green Knight, who rises and picks up his severed head.

Originally, Gawain's arrival at the Green Chapel to await the return blow would have taken place in six months, not a year, or both parties would in effect be representing the same god-type. When the moment of reckoning comes Gawain is spared by his rival, who only grazes his neck with the axe, just as the Green Knight was struck but did not die. Therefore, both the god of summer and of winter are 'resurrected' to fight again in due season.

Sources differ as to the bird associated with the holly, some giving the robin, others the wren, and there is a case for both. In Welsh myth the robin is said to have brought fire to mankind, burning its breast red as a result - consistent with the fire association of tinne/tan.

Irish tradition says that the wren (symbolizing the god of the waning year) was hiding in a holly bush when he was slain by the robin (god of the waxing year), his successor. This myth has been ritually enacted across continents and ages, from ancient Greece and Rome to South West England, Brittany, Wales, and present day Ireland. On either Christmas Eve, St Stephen's Day (26th December) or New Year's Day men would hunt and kill a wren, which was then carried in procession as a trophy to bring good luck. The fact that killing a wren at any other time was/is strictly taboo and thought to bring misfortune proves its ancient sanctity. Nowadays, the actual hunt to the death is sometimes avoided and the dead wren substituted by an effigy in the celebrations, just as a human victim was once substituted by the wren.

For Christians, as for Pagans, holly represents eternal life, with the red berries symbolizing the blood of sacrifice and the prickly leaves Christ's crown of thorns. One tradition claims that holly sprang up under Christ's feet when he walked in the world of men. The words holy and holly have the same root and both occur in place names, often with a dual meaning. For example Holyhead, on Holy Island, Anglesey, is pronounced 'Hollyhead'.

Though his birth around the Winter Solstice makes Jesus a representative of the waxing rather than the waning year, he has a strong link with holly through the theme of resurrection and the immortality of the soul, as shown in the following Medieval carol:

> *The holly she bears a berry, as blood it is red*
> *and we trust in our saviour who rose from the dead.*

The same carol also contains the chorus:

> *The first tree that's in the greenwood*
> *it was the holly.*

This acknowledgement of the tree's importance is echoed in the better known *'The Holly and the Ivy'*, which shares some of its lines with the above:

> *The holly and the ivy*
> *when they are both full-grown,*
> *of all the trees in the wood*
> *the holly bears the crown.*

The competition between holly and ivy stands for the battle of the sexes in English folk custom, according to Robert Graves. Ivy was generally seen as feminine, though it was also associated with Saturn, and in many traditions the nest/hiding place of his totem bird the wren was, not the holly, but the ivy. Holly, on the other hand, was seen as a masculine tree, and on Yule morning the first person to cross the threshold had to be a dark-haired man, Saturn's representative, who was given the title Holly Boy. Women were kept away at this time, causing rivalry, though contests between Ivy Girls and Holly Boys later became a festive Yuletide custom.

In *'The Mabinogion'* story *'The Tale of Taliesin'* Elffin's imprisonment by King Maelgwn of Gwynedd for boasting, and Taliesin's subsequent contest with the royal Chief Bard Heinin, takes place at Christmas. Later, when a horse race is arranged between Elffin's horse and twenty-four of Maelgwn's, Taliesin instructs the youth riding Elffin's horse to:

*'let all the king's horses get before him and as he should overtake one horse after the other, to take one of the twigs* (of holly) *and strike the horse with it.....and then let that twig fall.'*

The tale does not explain what this is meant to achieve though it may derive from a belief dating back to the Romans, and a statement by the writer Pliny, who claimed that if holly was thrown at an animal it would be compelled to return to the place where it was hit and lie down. Alternatively, Robert Graves believes that Maelgwn's twenty-four horses represent the final hours of the old year, ruled by the winter lord, which the Child of Light, the Mabon (symbolized by Taliesin) puts behind him before his rebirth at the Solstice.

The Irish Brehon Law names holly as a Chieftain because:

*'the axle-trees of chariots are made of it.'*[2]

Spear shafts, too, were made of holly wood which, combined with its natural defences, meant that holly became the symbolic tree of the warrior.

D W Nash's translation of the *'Cad Goddeu'* states:

*'The holly dark green,
He was very courageous:
Defended with spikes on every side,
Wounding the hands.'*[3]

The idea that holly is a strong defender continued in the folk belief that it offered protection against both physical and supernatural danger. It was once used as a charm against lightning and fire, in a kind of reverse logic stemming from its association with this element. In fact the wood burns easily, even when fresh, giving us the word 'tinder', a derivation of 'tinne'.

Holly also had a reputation for warding off evil: newborn infants were sprinkled with an infusion of its leaves, and witches and malevolent spirits were thought to be repelled by a holly hedge. Possibly because of the purgative action of the berries, a holly hedge was believed to guard against poisoning as well.

Though it is the tree of the waning year, holly is always seen as beneficial. Even when the berries represent the blood of sacrifice, it is Jesus' noble sacrifice for the good of mankind, or the god of the waning year's ritual death so that the old may give way to the new.

**Sources for quotes:**
1. Guest, Lady Charlotte (trans). - *'Mabinogion Legends'*.
2. Commissioners for Publishing the Ancient Laws and Institutes of Ireland - *'Ancient Laws of Ireland, Vol IV'*.
3. Nash, D W (trans.) *'Taliesin, or the Bards and Druids of Britain'*.

Green-armoured warrior,
Alban Hefin's victor,
King Wren on your shoulder.
Wielding thirteen sharp spears
on each leaf, to repel the attacker.

Winter sacrifice -
your berries drip blood red
from the tip of the Oak King's sword.
Released with the soul of the wren
your life flies on his wing
to the darkness of Annwn
till your season to rule
is upon us again.

# Holly Protection Rite

This rite can be performed if you are feeling threatened by another person, by their negative thoughts or actions, and is also suitable for helping to overcome a sense of fear, either general or specific. It must not be used as a form of psychic attack against anyone, but should focus on the defensive qualities of the holly only.

Find a mature holly bush and speak the holly greeting given above, or one of your own devising. If you sense the holly spirit's acceptance of your request to work with it, after asking permission cut several small sprigs for your sacred space, leaving a suitable offering in return.

Lay your altar or table with either a dark green or a berry-red cloth, together with incense and candles. Place the sprigs of holly on it, along with any other relevant symbols such as the Wood Wisdom holly card, an image of the Green Knight, wren, robin or an Ogham stave.

If you wish, cast a circle and request the presence of the elemental powers in the four quarters.

Pick up one of the holly sprigs and, still holding it, sit calmly to journey through the gate onto the woodland path. After closing the gate firmly behind you, continue walking between the trees until you come to a holly bush, bright with scarlet berries. Pause for a moment in contemplation, then say:

*'I ask that your spirit be present with me here in this sacred space.'*

Wait for the spirit of the holly to appear to your inner eye, in whatever form. For example, when I performed the rite it took the appearance of a Celtic warrior carrying a holly-shafted spear and a red shield with a holly device, and with a sword at his belt.

Ask if the spirit is willing to help you, and if so say:

*'I request your protection against all harmful influences, negative thoughts and intrusions on all planes: spiritual, mental and physical. For myself, my home and all those close to me.'*

If there are any more specific details, state them clearly. It is also important to say, and mean, the following:

*'I ask you to defend, never to attack. I seek only harmony and understanding. Should negative thoughts or actions be directed against me I wish you to deflect them with your strong shield, in peace.'*

Again, as an example I include the reply I received from the holly warrior that I made contact with:

*'It is my way only to act in defence. My shield will be a shield to protect you, your home and dear ones. My spear will be like the bar of a gate which cannot be passed. My sword will be a bridge which may not be crossed.'* He drew it and held it high. *'I swear that I will do as you ask.'*

When you have finished your communication, offer thanks and promise to always honour and respect the holly. Return via the woodland gate, but before opening your eyes visualize the holly spirit standing beside you, surrounded by a clear radiant light that also surrounds you and your home like shining armour.

Finally, give thanks to the holly spirit and the elemental powers, then unwind the circle.

Keep the sprigs of holly in a safe place, or secure them over your front door. In a few days, weeks or months time, whenever you no longer feel fearful, perform a second rite to offer thanks, as the aim of the initial rite has now been achieved, and burn the holly sprigs. It is disrespectful simply to forget that you called for help, not to acknowledge a spirit who has worked for you and bring your association to a formal close.

A secluded pool is encircled by a thicket, rich with clusters of nuts:


Hazel, Coll, Collen,
gentle, secret one,
inspiration's gift.
Revealer of bardic truth,
I come in peace and in search of wisdom.
My greetings and blessings to you and all your kin.
Is it your wish to share your knowledge and energy with me?

# Hazel

The hazel (*Corylus avellana*) is a bushy tree that produces multiple branches at its base, though it can develop a single trunk and reach a height of 10m if not coppiced. It has reddish-brown bark, and broad hairy leaves with a ragged edge which begin to unfurl in April, around the time of flowering. Immature male catkins are visible on the bare branches throughout the winter, lengthening into long lambs' tails in spring, while the green female buds, also visible during winter, develop into clusters of nuts which are ripe in September.

Hazel is common in hedgerows and woodland throughout Europe, especially in oak woods where it forms a shrub layer. It has great power to regenerate when coppiced, ie. cut back to ground level, and its long pliable twigs are harvested for basket and hurdle-weaving.

The Medieval Irish Brehon Law defines hazel as one of the seven Chieftain trees because of:

*'its nuts and its wattles.'*[1]

It can also be used to dowse for underground features or buried objects, the dowser carrying a forked twig that reacts (usually with a downward pull) to the presence of water, metal, etc. Until the seventeenth century a similar method of divination was thought to reveal if a man was guilty of a crime.

Mythologically, hazel is the supreme tree of wisdom in Celtic tradition, held in such reverence that the Triads of Ireland, which pre-date the Brehon Law, place it amongst the three 'unbreathing things' - along with the apple tree and a sacred grove - whose destruction must be paid for with 'breathing things', probably referring to the death penalty.

The Irish myth *'The Adventures of Cormac in the Land of*

**101**

*Promise'* tells how the king visits the sea god Manannan MacLir's Otherworldly palace, where he sees a fountain with five streams flowing from it. Nine hazel trees grow above the fountain and whenever the nuts fall into the pool they are eaten by the five salmon swimming there.

Manannan interprets Cormac's vision, saying that the five streams represent the five senses, and that poetic wisdom is obtained by drinking both from the fountain - the source of knowledge - and from the five streams.

A further connection between hazel, wisdom and water occurs in the Irish Dindsenchas (place name tales), which describe Connla's Well, as surrounded by hazels of inspiration, science and poetry. Again, the nuts are eaten by salmon.

Wisdom was concentrated in the nuts that fell into Connla's Well at the source of the river Boyne or, according to other accounts, of the River Shannon. Because the salmon developed a spot on their backs for each nut consumed, by extension all salmon, with their spotted scales, came to symbolize wisdom. The passage about Connla's Well also describes how the trees around it flowered and fruited simultaneously - the flowers symbolic of beauty, the nuts of wisdom. Just as the initiate's power is closely guarded and not won without effort, so the tough hazel shell protects the sweet edible kernel within - wisdom itself.

Both the Shannon and the Boyne are sacred rivers, associated respectively with the goddesses Sinend and Boann. Through the hazels growing over the well at the source of the river, and the salmon swimming in its depths, the goddess of inspiration bestows her gift on the Bard.

In Celtic belief water sources were not only linked with goddesses, but regarded as entrances to the Otherworld, from where the hazel drew its spiritual power, and votive offerings were made by dropping the nuts into pools and wells.

The hero most closely connected with the Salmon of Wisdom is the Irish shamanic warrior Fionn MacCumhaill:

His father, leader of the Fianna, is killed before Fionn's birth and the infant is given to two wise-women for fostering, at this time still bearing his childhood name of Deimne. He only acquires the name Fionn ('Fair One') as a youth after defeating some other youths at hurly. When they complain to their lord, describing the stranger who has beaten them, the lord declares that he shall be called Fionn from that day on.

Following further adventures Fionn kills Liath, the man who struck the first fatal blow against his father, and retrieves the crane bag which Liath had stolen from Cumhaill. This crane bag was originally Manannan's and contains the secrets of the bardic tradition from the Otherworld, Manannan's realm beneath the waves.

Fionn then becomes apprentice to the Druid Finn Eces ('White Wisdom') in order to protect himself from being slain by Liath's clan, as they would be unlikely to risk forfeiting the large honour price payable for the killing of a Bard. Finn Eces believes he is destined to find and eat the Salmon of Wisdom, and has been fishing for seven years at Fec's pool on the Boyne when he eventually catches it and gives it to Fionn to cook. However, while it is roasting over a spit some hot fish oil spatters onto the youth's thumb which he puts in his mouth to cool, immediately receiving inspiration. Finn Eces wisely allows him to eat the remainder, accepting that it was the boy, not himself, who was destined to gain supreme knowledge.

The Welsh *'Mabinogion' 'Tale of Taliesin'* has many parallels to that of Fionn. In the story, the goddess Cerridwen brews up a cauldron containing a magical elixir, hoping to bestow wisdom on her son Avagddu to compensate for his ugliness. As the brew must simmer for a year and a day she employs a young boy named Gwion to stir it but, like Fionn, he puts his finger in his mouth when a droplet splashes out, thus gaining the poetic wisdom apparently meant for another.

After an initiatory shape-shifting sequence Gwion is re-born as the great Bard Taliesin, whom Cerridwen places in a leather bag and leaves to the mercy of the waves. Later, the bag is washed up at a weir in place of the haul of salmon expected by Elffin (nephew to King Maelgwn of Gwynedd), who adopts the boy.

Though there is no reference to salmon eating hazel nuts in Welsh myth as it exists today, it may originally have been mentioned in a lost fragment or tale. Perhaps hazel was even one of the magical ingredients in Ceridwen's elixir of inspiration. The similarity between the two stories certainly indicates a common set of beliefs, if not one root myth: both deal with the sacred nature of the salmon, the names Gwion and Fionn both mean 'Fair One', and inspiration comes via water - the pool or cauldron.

Like Fionn and Taliesin, Aengus Og, the Irish god of love, symbolizes wisdom in youth, a quality represented by the hazel wand he carries. The theme of wise youth and the bardic power of the hazel also occurs in the Irish 'Colloquy of Two Sages' when Nede, a young Fili (poet), contends for the chair of Ollave (the highest poetic grade). During a series of magical questions he replies to the elder Fili, Ferchertne, that he knows the hazels of poetry.

Hazel is generally seen as beneficial, though Irish myth shows this is not always the case - that every light casts its shadow. In the second Battle of Magh Tuiredh, fought for dominion of Ireland, Balor, the Fomorian god, is slain by Lugh of the Tuatha de Danaan. His head is then placed in the fork of a hazel tree on White Hazel Mountain, which splits in two, its sap turning to poison. Manannan orders the Dripping Hazel to be felled, and when the shield made from its wood is later carried by Fionn it emits toxic fumes that kill thousands of his enemies in battle, symbolic either of the satirical poem employed by the ancient Bards, or perhaps of knowledge misused. The price of seeking wisdom for the wrong ends is emphasized in a myth which tells how Balor lost the sight of one eye after an enchanted potion splashed into it as he watched a group of Druids brewing a cauldron of inspiration.

The hazel, and its associated water source, are again linked with mystic inspiration in Geoffrey of Monmouth's 'Vita Merlini', which contains a description of Merlin's solitary refuge in the wilds of Coed Celyddon, on the summit of a mountain where there is a fountain surrounded by hazel bushes. Here, Merlin lives the life of a shaman, experiencing prophetic visions as a result of being traumatized by the Battle of Arderydd. The entranced poet as diviner, foretelling the future, takes us back to the diviner who, searching for an object or answer, uses a hazel rod to gain knowledge of hidden truths.

To drink from the cauldron or sacred fountain, or to partake of the salmon who swim in the pool, feeding on the hazels that fall into its waters, is to tap the fount of Bright Knowledge sought by the ancient Bards.

**Sources for quotes:**
1. Commissioners for Publishing the Ancient Laws and Institutes of Ireland - *'Ancient Laws of Ireland, Vol IV'*.

Three times three
the hazel trees
grow round the sacred fountain.
Five salmon leaping,
nine shells cracking;
strong caskets of wisdom
unlocked. Treasure tasted
in every sweet kernel
a spot of royal purple
on a silver scaled back.


Three times round
Connla's Well
Boann span in trance.
The waters sighed
and roared in rage,
they foamed and surged
in rising waves.
Waves breaking over her,
waves at one with her -
in a river of life.


From Shannon's shore
and Boyne's banks,
in Connla's Well
and Manannan's land,
west of the sunset,
beyond the ninth wave,
seekers of wisdom hunt
swift, spotted salmon:
keepers of knowledge -
dream-feast of Bards.

Seven years waiting,
long seasons searching,
the sacred fish speared
by Finn Eces hand:
hazel-wise treasure
in a silvery skin,
one taste to bring
bright inspiration,
knowledge of all things.


Fire flames dancing,
sacred catch roasting,
watched over by Fionn,
MacCumhaill's son.
Fish scented smoke and
rich oil spitting,
the moment approaches
to swallow and know,
the Bard Finn Eces'
life-quest done.


Summer wind gusting,
fanned flames rising,
a drop of hot oil
strikes Fionn's thumb.
With a cry he thrusts
it into his mouth.
Elixir on his tongue;
in a flash of vision
the apprentice has won
his master's wisdom.

# Rite of Bardic Eloquence

Decorate your sacred space, with hazel boughs, candles, incense and any other items that you feel are appropriate. Also place a chalice of fresh spring water and a dish of hazel nuts on the altar/table.

If you wish, cast a sacred circle and ask the blessings of the elements in the four quarters.

Then stand facing the altar and say:

> *Inspiration: deep as the Well of Wisdom.*
> *Memory: clear as the sacred spring.*
> *Eloquence: flowing as the mighty river.*
> *These gifts I seek,*
> *if it be the will of the gods*
> *and for the good of all.*

Sit quietly, still facing the altar, to undertake an inner journey. Pass through the gate onto the woodland path, and continue until you come to a circle of hazel bushes, surrounding a natural spring which flows into a clear pool. As you look into its depths, meditating on your reason for being in this place, you see the reflection of a man wearing the robes of a Bard, and raise your eyes, recognising the figure beside you.

Address him in these words, or words of your own:

> *Chief Bard Taliesin, I give you honour.*
> *Master of bardic wisdom,*
> *strong in the power of speech,*
> *weaver of living words,*
> *I request your guidance in my search for inspiration and eloquence.*

Walk with Taliesin sunwise around the pool, or sit beside one of the hazel bushes as you listen to the wisdom he has to impart. You fel the strength of his presence beside you, giving you confidence, and the energies of the sacred pool and hazel circle filling you with inspiration.

As Taliesin speaks, you watch the salmon rise to the surface of the pool, eat three hazel nuts that fall into it, and disappear again into its depths. When you raise your eyes you find that Taliesin is no longer visible, though you can still sense his presence and know that he can hear you as you give thanks.

When you fel ready, retrace the path through the woodland to the gate, close it behind you and return to ordinary consciousness.

Standing in front of the altar, hold your forefinger or wand (see willow chapter) over the chalice of spring water and say:

> *Lord Manannan, guardian of the sacred fountain where the salmon of wisdom swim, I ask your blessings on this water. The outer symbol of the inner reality, I drink wisdom and inspiration into myself.*

Take a draught and pause, feeling its power. After a moment, hold you forefinger or wand over the dish of hazel nuts and say:

> *Lord Manannan, guardian of the sacred fountain where the hazels of poetry grow, I ask your blessings on these nuts. The outer symbol of the inner reality, I drink wisdom and inspiration into myself.*

Eat three nuts, feeling the bardic inspiration and eloquence within you, and visualize yourself sharing it through story telling, poetry or song. Then give thanks to Manannan and Taliesin and to the elemental powers before unwinding the circle.

Leave the rest of the hazel nuts in the garden or out in nature, and sprinkle the remaining water on the earth as an offering.

Mellow sunlight fills an orchard of crooked, lichen-covered trees, their branches heavy with the autumn's yield.


Apple, Quert, Afal,
covered in fragrant blossom,
or bearing fruit, sharp and sweet.
Tree of immortality,
I come in peace and in search of wisdom.
My greetings and blessings to you and all your kin.
Is it your wish to share your knowledge and energy with me?

# Apple

The crab apple (*Malus sylvestris*) is native to the British Isles and occurs in hedgerows and woodland throughout Europe, except in the far north. According to recent research it is not a close genetic relative of the cultivated apple (*Malus domestica*), which was introduced to Britain by the Romans as an orchard tree but can now be found naturalized in the wild.

The leaves of both wild and domestic trees unfurl in May or June, around the same time as the blossoms appear. In autumn, the crab apple produces sour yellowish fruit which is half the diameter of the sweet-tasting eating apple. There have been over 6,000 kinds of cultivated apple grown in Britain over the years, though today many are rare or lost, abandoned in favour of the main commercial varieties. Evocative names from around the country include: Royal George, Fair Maid of Taunton, Sweet Russet Coat, Small Cats Head, Whittles Dumpling, Cornish Honeypin, Tower of Glamis and Kentish Fillbasket.

Some communities celebrate Apple Day on the nearest weekend to 21st October, in an attempt to save old varieties by re-awakening interest, and to preserve traditional customs associated with apples. The ancient practice of Wassailing apple trees also continues, or has been revived, in many places, including Glastonbury, linked with the mythical Isle of Avalon. On 17th January, old New Year's Day, a Wassailing ceremony is performed at the Rural Life Museum, where the company gathers beneath the oldest tree - said to be the home of the Apple-Tree Man, guardian spirit of the orchard. A shotgun is fired into the branches 'to scare away evil spirits', and an offering of toast soaked in cider is placed amongst them before a traditional Wassailing song is sung, its chorus carrying a memory of Pagan chants for fertility:

'Bud and blossom, bud and blossom, bud and bloom and bear,
So we may have plenty and cider all next year.

*Hatfuls and in capfuls and bushel-bags and all,*
*And the cider running out of every gutter-hole.'*

To the Celts the apple was one of the most sacred of trees, and classified as a Chieftain under the Medieval Brehon Law because of:

*'its fruit and its bark;'[1]*

which can be used for tanning leather. The earlier Triads of Ireland show its high status, equal to a hazel bush or a sacred grove, by warning that the destruction of these 'unbreathing things' must be paid for only by 'breathing things', implying that the penalty for felling them is death.

The reason for this becomes clear when we examine the role played by the apple in mythology, where it is described as a tree of the Otherworld, beauty and immortality. Several Irish Immrama, spiritual voyages undertaken in search of Paradise or the Otherworld, mention apples which possess magical powers or apple trees which fruit and flower simultaneously.

St. Brendan is inspired to travel after hearing the words of the holy man Barinthus:

*'And when we had entered the boat a mist fell upon us.......And when we had spent the space of an hour of the day in this way.......we saw the island in resplendent beauty, full of fragrant apples and blossom; and there was no single herb or tree among them which was not laden with fruit.'[2]*

Later, Barinthus and his son Merroc meet a hermit on the island who tells them:

*'And ye need no food or drink; for ye have been a year in this land and have not tasted food or drink all that time, and further ye have not needed rest or sleep, nor has night or other darkness befallen you.'[3]*

Another Celtic traveller, Maildun, sets out not in search of Paradise but in order to track down the plunderers who killed his father. When they are starving the crew of his curragh come upon an island with a single glorious apple tree and Maildun clasps a low-hanging branch:

*'For three days and three nights......he held the branch, letting it slide through his hand, till on the third day he found a cluster of seven apples on the very end. Each of these apples supplied the travellers with food and drink for forty days and forty nights.'*

Apples with magical properties are again encountered in *'The Voyage of the Sons of O'Corra'*, which tells how three young men repent of their violent past and undertake a pilgrimage to the west:

*'They rowed forward for a long time till there was shown to them a wonderful island, and in it a great grove of marvellous beauty, laden with apples, golden coloured and sweet scented. A sparkling rivulet of wine flowed through the midst of the grove; and when the wind blew through the trees, sweeter than any music was the rustling it made. The O'Corras ate some of the apples and drank from the rivulet of wine, and were immediately satisfied. And from that time forth they were never troubled by either wounds or sickness.*[3]

Such descriptions are reminiscent of the mystic Isle of Avalon (etymologically associated with the Welsh for apple - Afal), where the dying King Arthur is carried after the Battle of Camlann. Avalon can also be related to the ancient Greek Elysian Fields, paradisiacal abode of the blessed dead.

In *'The History of the Kings of Britain'*, written in the first half of the twelfth century, Geoffrey of Monmouth tells us that the mortally wounded King Arthur was taken to the Isle of Avalon for his wounds to be attended to. Earlier, he mentions that Arthur's sword Caliburn (Excalibur) was forged on the Isle of Avalon, implying that it is a weapon of supernatural power.

Thomas Malory's *'Le Morte D'Arthur'* (completed c.1470) spells Avalon 'Avilion', though in all other respects his more detailed description of Arthur's last journey agrees with Geoffrey's:

*'Now put me into the barge, said the king. And he* (Sir Bedivere) *did so softly; and there received him three queens with great mourning.......... Then Sir Bedivere cried: Ah my lord Arthur, what shall become of me, now ye go from me and leave me here alone among mine enemies? Comfort thyself, said the king........for I will into the Vale of Avilion to heal me of my grievous wound.'*[4]

Other Celtic tales recount how an apple or apple bough is brought to this world by a faery being in order to lure mortals to the Otherworld. For example, in *'Connla of the Golden Hair and the Fairy Maiden'* Connla is approached by a beautiful lady who declares that she is in love with him and wishes him to go with her to the 'Land of the Living'. Connla's father Conn summons his Druid to banish her, but as she vanishes she throws an enchanted apple to the prince so that:

*'Connla remained for a whole month without tasting food or drink, except the apple. And though he ate of it each day, it was never lessened, but was as whole and perfect in the end as at the beginning.'*[3]

Later, when the druidic banishing has lost its power:

*'the king observed, and marvelled greatly, that whenever the lady was present his son never spoke one word to anyone, nay, even though they addressed him many times.'*[3]

Finally, Connla leaves Ireland to accompany his love to the Otherworld in a crystal curragh, never to be seen again.

A similar theme runs through the tale *'The Voyage of*

*Bran mac Fabel to the Land of Faery'*. After a mysterious woman has appeared at the royal hall, Bran is out walking alone when he is lulled to sleep by enchanting music. He wakes to find a silver branch with white blossoms near to where he is lying and carries it back to the hall. The faery woman then appears again before the company, singing the following verses:

> '*A branch of the apple tree from Emain
> I bring, like those we know;
> Twigs of white silver are on it
> Crystal grows with blossoms.*[5]

Once she has spoken she vanishes, taking the branch with her, though having held it Bran can no longer live contentedly in the mortal realm and follows the woman to the Otherworld. He lives there for what he believes to be a year, but upon returning to his kingdom he finds that centuries have gone by and that all his family and comrades are long dead.

Historically, an Irish Filli (Bard) who had undergone seven to nine years training was entitled to carry a silver branch as a symbol of office, while an Ollave (the highest grade of Filli) carried a branch of gold and a lesser Bard one of bronze. The branch, which was hung with bells, would be shaken before the Filli began to speak, the power of his eloquence transporting his hearers to the Otherworld. The symbolism of the bardic silver or golden branch is explained by tales such as *'The Voyage of Bran mac Fabel to the Land of Faery'* which show the link with the magical apple trees that grow in the Otherworld - source of inspiration. Though in the above version of the story there are blossoms but no apples on the branch, in others it is said to bear silver apples.

In Welsh tradition apple symbolism is found in *'The Mabinogion'* tale *'The Dream of Rhonabwy'*. After falling asleep on an ox hide, a method frequently employed by the ancient Druids to attain trance states, Rhonabwy experiences a strange vision in which he meets King Arthur and a number of heroes from Brythonic myth. As a prelude to a game of gwyddbwyll, a form of chess, between Arthur and Owain, a man spreads a mantle with a red-gold apple in each corner on the ground and places Arthur's chair on it.

The whole tale, with its weird and vivid descriptions of colour, is clearly a journey to the Otherworld, confirmed by the presence of the apples on the mantle. The game, too, is highly symbolic, with each move made by the players paralleled by Arthur's men and Owain's ravens attacking each other.

Another *'Mabinogion'* tale *'Kilhwch and Olwen'* also mentions apples decorating the corners of a mantle, this time worn by the hero as he sets off on his quest to win the hand of Olwen - a quest that leads him into the Otherworld in the company of heroes who possess superhuman shamanic powers:

*'About him was a four-cornered cloth of purple, and an apple of gold was at each corner; and every one of the apples was of the value of an hundred kine.'*[6]

The bardic poem *'Afallennau'* (Apple Trees) is transcribed in 'The Black Book of Carmarthen', dated to around 1250 but containing material of far greater age. Here Myrddin is the shaman and mad prophet of Geoffrey of Monmouth's *'Vita Merlini'* rather than the dignified wizard, Merlin, of the later Arthurian romances. After being driven to the brink of insanity by the battle of Arderydd, he takes refuge in Coed Celyddon where he shelters beneath an apple tree, addressing prophetic verses to it.

Myrddin shows deep reverence for the tree, which forms a bridge between this world and the Other, aiding him to enter a state of trance. Nor does the tree itself belong entirely to the physical realm, as Myrddin believes it will conceal him from his enemies.

The true reason for the apple's mythological association with the Otherworld is lost in the mists of time, though it may have arisen because apples are in season around Samhain,

**119**

the Celtic feast of the dead.

In the fairytale '*Snow White*', the apple is linked with initiation, when the heroine is tricked into accepting a 'poisoned' apple. Though she cannot be roused after eating it, she still appears to be alive, so the dwarfs do not bury her but place her in a glass casket. When a prince then buys it from them and has it borne away, the piece of apple lodged in Snow White's mouth falls out and she revives. The symbolism of the tale indicates that the apple was not literally poisoned but that by eating it Snow White entered the Otherworld in a state of trance, bringing about her initiation into womanhood or enlightened freedom. After a period of darkness/restriction, first as despised step-daughter, then as unpaid housekeeper to the dwarfs, she awakens to both inner and outer riches when she marries the prince.

Most widely known of all tales involving the apple is the biblical account of Adam and Eve, though ironically, given the area where the story originated, the fruit of temptation may well not have been an apple but a fig or date. The Bible does not say what species symbolizes the Tree of Knowledge of Good and Evil, but after a translation by Aquila of Pontus in the second century AD identified it as apple the belief has become established, probably due to the number of western myths in which apple trees were associated with an otherworldly paradise. And Robert Graves points out that the apple represents consummation in European folklore.

Descriptions of the Garden of Eden are certainly similar to those of the Pagan Otherworld as found in Celtic and classical myth:

'And out of the ground made the Lord God to grow every tree that is pleasant to the sight, and good for food; the Tree of Life also in the midst of the garden, and the Tree of Knowledge of Good and Evil.'

Amongst such beauty Adam and Eve exist in immortal bliss, obeying God's command:

'The Tree of the Knowledge of Good and Evil, thou shalt not eat of it: for in the day that thou eatest thereof thou shalt surely die.'

However, after the serpent persuades Eve to defy the command, promising that the forbidden fruit will bring great wisdom, she in turn persuades Adam to taste it. With universal understanding comes the understanding of carnal love so, as all creatures who reproduce must die to make way for their off-spring, by eating from the Tree of Knowledge the couple become mortal. Yet, if they were to eat from the Tree of Life they would regain their immortality:

'And the Lord God said, Behold, the man is become as one of us, to know good and evil: and now, lest he put forth his hand, and take also of the Tree of Life, and eat, and life for ever:
'Therefore the Lord God sent him forth from the garden of Eden, to till the ground from whence he was taken.'

Reminiscent of the biblical serpent, the dragon Ladon guards the Golden Apples of the Hesperides in Greek mythology - the symbolism of serpent and dragon being closely linked and often interchangeable. One of the twelve labours of Hercules is to find the Golden Apples, which were given to the goddess Juno as a wedding present and placed in the safekeeping of the Hesperides, the three daughters of Hesperus, lord of the west. Though the tale says that the apples are hidden in Africa, this name is often used to describe any distant land, and the connection with Hesperus locates the apples in the traditional direction of the Otherworld.

Another Greek myth, the famous tale of the Trojan War, begins with the wedding feast of Thetis and Peleus, to which all the gods are invited except Eris, the goddess of discord. Furious, she makes an appearance and places a golden apple on the feast table, its inscription 'to the fairest' causing bitter rivalry amongst the goddesses, who all believe they should be awarded the prize. Finally, the other contenders back down, leaving only Hera, Athene and Aphrodite. As none of the guests are willing to take the consequences of pronouncing a judgement, it falls to Paris, who unsurprisingly chooses Aphrodite, goddess of love and beauty. His choice is also influenced by her promise of a bride as lovely as herself if he declares her the winner. Paris then sets his sights on Helen, the greatest beauty of her time, and seduces her away from her husband, Menelaus, resulting in war between Greece and Troy. A theme of strife replaces the more usual otherworldly journey, but the apple's association with youth, beauty and love echoes that of the Celtic tales.

Similar symbolism occurs in Norse myth, with the apples belonging to the goddess Idun possessing the power to bestow immortal youth and beauty on anyone who eats them. After her marriage to Braggi, lord of poetry and song, Idun accompanies him to the divine realm of Asgard, where she allows the gods to feast on the apples each day, though however many are consumed the number in her casket remains the same. Because the Norse gods are not all naturally immortal, the magical apples are invaluable to them, and are also coverted by other beings such as dwarfs and giants.

In one tale, whilst Braggi is absent Idun is tricked away from Asgard by Loki and captured by the storm giant Thiassi. She remains in his bleak realm until the gods, beginning to feel their strength ebbing away and old age coming upon them, force Loki to find a means of rescuing Idun and her treasured fruit. Symbolically, her absence in the land of the storm giant represents winter when nature dies, while her return in spring brings life and beauty back to the earth.

The otherworldly apple tree apparently offers all that god or mortal may desire, but that gift does not come without a price as many tales show. The magic apple can also teach a harsh lesson.

## Sources for quotes:
1. Commissioners for Publishing the Ancient Laws and Institutes of Ireland - *'Ancient Laws of Ireland, Vol IV'*.
2. MacDonald, Iain (ed.) - *'Saint Brendan'*, Floris Books, Edinburgh, 1992. Original source - Plummer, Charles (trans) *'Life of St Brendan'*, 1922.
3. Joyce, P W - 'Old Celtic Romances', Wordsworth Editions, Ware, Herts, 2000. Original edition published by David Nutt & Co, 1907.
4. Malory, Sir Thomas - *Le Morte D'Arthur*, Wordsworth, Ware, Herts, 1996.
5. Matthews, John - *'Taliesin'*. Original source - Meyer, Kuno - *'The Voyage of Bran son of Febal*, D Nutt, 1895.
6. Guest, Charlotte (trans.) - *'Mabinogion Legends'*.

# The Bard's Vision

Nine waves
beyond the shore,
I see the Plain of Honey.
Sweet golden mead
flows from its fountains.
And a tree of bright aspect,
glorious to behold.
Three fruits upon it:
nuts, apples and acorns.
Three birds of jewelled plumage
sing Rhiannon's song,
the song Bran heard
with the noble company
living ever-young
on the Isle of Glass.
A tree on a plain,
of silver, of gold,
crowned in sun,
roots held fast
in the realm of Arawn.

# The Apple - Fun, Fantasy, and Folk Games

The majority of traditional games involving apples are played at Hallowe'en, the Celtic feast of Samhain, when the veil between our world and the Otherworld is thin, making it an appropriate time for divination.

In magical practice the apple is the perfect offering for the gods around Samhain and its many associations provide rich symbolism for meditation and inner journeying. But it is important to make a connection with any sacred tree on as many levels as possible, and with the apple all the senses can be enlivened: sight - by the vivid colours and contrasts; taste - not only by eating fresh apples, but by drinking cider and trying seasonal recipes; smell - by noticing that all parts of the tree, including sap and leaves, have a faint apple scent. And there can be nothing more evocative of autumn than the heady aroma of fallen apples as they begin to rot and ferment; sound - by listening to the music of the wind as it swishes through the leaves of an orchard, as the sons of O'Corra did; and touch - by feeling the wonderful texture to be found on the bark of an ancient tree.

Playing traditional games, many with a symbolic meaning, is another way of working with the apple on the earth plane, creating a sense of community as winter nights draw in, as well as stimulating the five senses.

### Apple Bobbing

Place a number of apples in a tub/washing-up bowl filled with water and ask the players to take turns at retrieving one, using only their teeth. Each player is allowed three attempts. As a contest, see who can catch the most apples, or the largest. As a form of fortune telling, large apples can symbolize wealth, small ones or failing to retrieve one at all, poverty.

Alternatively, float the apples as before, but each participant must hold a fork in his/her mouth and try to stab an apple with it, or hold the fork by hand and drop it on an apple in the hope of spearing it.

## Bob Apple

For this game attach an apple to a piece of string, hang it from a stick and swung it round. One player at a time, or several at once, must then try to take a bite of apple without touching it with their hands.

## Pass the Apple

In this team game the participants stand in a line and pass an apple from chin to chin, again without using their hands. The team whose apple reaches the end of the line first is the winner, though if the apple falls as it is being passed it must be returned to the start of the line.

## Fortune telling with Apples

In folk magic apples were often used for divination in matters of love and choice, recalling the tale of Paris and the golden apple in Greek myth. Traditionally, love divination was performed by girls looking for a husband or choosing between suitors, but times change.

Method 1: Twist the apple stalk whilst reciting the alphabet, and the letter at which it breaks off is your future partner's first initial. To find the second initial, stab the apple with the stalk, again reciting the alphabet, until the skin is pierced.

Method 2: Peel an apple and throw the peel over your shoulder. If it lands in the shape of a letter, that is the initial of your future partner.

Method 3: Take the pips from an apple and throw them

in the fire, saying the names of possible partners. If a pip bursts, the person whose name you were saying at the time is the one!


### Recipe - Toffee Apples
* Wash 8 apples and remove stalks.
* Push a skewer or wooden chopstick into each.
* Put 450g/1lb granulated sugar and 150ml/5 fl. oz water in a sturdy pan and stir until the sugar has dissolved.
* Boil until the liquid is a golden colour, but do not over-boil or toffee will not set.
* Remove pan from heat and dip apples into toffee.
* Place apples on an oiled baking tray to cool.
* Eat and enjoy.

On a warm, south-facing wall a graceful plant weaves and climbs, its purple grapes catching the sunlight.


Vine, Muinn, Gwinwydden,
beauty of luscious fruit,
bounty of flowing wine.
Ecstatic, transforming spirit,
I come in peace and in search of wisdom.
My greetings and blessings to you and all your kin.
Is it your wish to share your knowledge and energy with me?

# Vine

The vine (*Vitis vinafera*) grows best in warm, sunny climates and on well-drained soil, though it can be cultivated outdoors in southern Britain. It is able to live for 600 years and produces branches that are strong and woody, up to 15 inches across in older plants. The tendrils that grow from the base of the leaves support the vine by curling around objects, giving it its name, which derives from 'viere' - 'to twist'. Clusters of small greenish flowers with a strong fragrance appear in summer and develop into grapes, used in wine-making since the earliest recorded times.

The vine is not mentioned in the Irish Brehon Law classification of sacred trees, probably because it is not native to the British Isles and is unable to survive in the wild in colder areas. However, as distinctive vine imagery is found in Bronze Age art, it must have been introduced to Britain at least two thousand years before the Roman Conquest. In his tree calendar Robert Graves allocates it to September, the month of the Autumn Equinox, when the grapes are ripe.

According to classical belief the vine was sacred to Dionysus (Greek)/Bacchus (Roman), a deity who represents the sacrificed and resurrected god-type, seen in mythology worldwide. Symbolically, he dies when the grapes are harvested and lives again as his spirit is transmuted into wine. The tales tell how Dionysus/BAcchus was accompanied by an intoxicated retinue of men, women, fauns, nymphs and satyrs, and that he rode in a chariot drawn by wild animals or was carried by his followers as he travelled the world, teaching mankind how to cultivate the vine and make wine from its fruit.

His association with fertility and abundance is evoked in a verse by the first century BC poet, Virgil:

'Come, sacred sire, with luscious clusters crown'd,
Here all the riches of thy reign abound;

*Each field replete with blushing autumn glows,*
*and in deep tides for thee the foaming vintage flows.*[1]

Dionysus/Bacchus, was one of the most popular deities of the classical world, whose festivals included the Greater and Lesser Dionysia, the Liberalia and the Bacchanalia. These involved orgiastic rites and wild dances, with the god's human followers emulating his mythological retinue, driven to the point of insanity from a combination of intoxicants and spiritual possession.

The tale of Pentheus, King of Thebes, shows a dark and ancient manifestation of such rites. After the herald sent to announce Dionysus' arrival at the gates of the city is dismissed, and the god told he must remain outside because of his riotous companions, Dionysus causes the Theban women to be overtaken by ecstatic frenzy. In this state they take part in the Mysteries celebrated in his honour, watched by the curious Pentheus who is concealed nearby. When a slight movement betrays the king's presence, his own mother Agave leads the intoxicated women as they haul him from his hiding place and tear his body to pieces.

A similar myth tells how the Bard Orpheus comes upon a group of Dionysian revellers after his failed attempt to rescue his wife Euridice from the Underworld. He is asked to perform a merry tune for them, but in his grief-stricken state is only able to play melancholy music. The celebrants are so enraged that Orpheus is torn apart and the pieces of his body thrown into the River Hebrus, his head repeating Euridice's name as it floats downstream to the Underworld.

According to some traditions, Dionysus himself was torn limb from limb, hinting that the tales of Orpheus and Pentheus are describing the ancient sacrifice of human victims, sacred kings, who took on the spirit of Dionysus and whose mutilated bodies were scattered on the fields to promote fertility. Though Plutarch (c.AD 46-126), who was himself a Delphic priest, states that initiates of the Orphic cult used the god's dismemberment as a metaphor for Dionysus' presence in many diverse forms: in the stars, elements, plants and animals.

Like Dionysus, the Egyptian god Osiris symbolized the cycle of death and rebirth in nature, more specifically in the sowing and harvesting of crops; also like Dionysus, after his murder by Set his body was broken into many pieces. Egyptian mythology describes how he was the first to pick fruit from trees, to cultivate the vine and to tread grapes. In order to teach all mankind the benefits of civilization and agriculture he then travelled the world, leaving Egypt in the hands of his wife, Isis. Throughout his travels he shared his knowledge of wine making with many nations, and where conditions made it impossible to grow the vine, Osiris taught the people how to brew beer from barley as a substitute.

Osiris' association with the vine is illustrated in the papyrus of Nebseni, which dates to around 1550 BC and shows the god seated in a shrine beneath a roof hung with clusters of grapes. The papyrus of Nekht shares this symbolism in its depiction of Osiris enthroned by a pool, surrounded by vines heavy with fruit.

The Bible describes the vine as one of the first plants to be cultivated after the waters of the great flood subsided, the only one mentioned by name:

*'And Noah began to be an husbandman, and he planted a vineyard: And he drank of the wine, and was drunken......'*

In the New Testament, Jesus addresses his disciples, saying,

*'I am the vine and you are the branches.'*

Later, during the Last Supper, he again uses vine/wine symbolism, inspiring the rite of Holy Communion:

*'And he took the cup, and gave thanks, and gave it to them, saying, Drink ye all of it;*
*'For this is my blood of the new testament, which is shed*

*for many for the remission of sins.*

*'But I say unto you, I will not drink henceforth of this fruit of the vine, until that day when I drink it new with you in my Father's kingdom.'*

This passage brings us back to the theme of the dying and resurrected god, and his link with the vine in many ancient cultures. Christ's blood, as symbolized by the wine, is offered to bring eternal life to the souls of mankind, and he refers to wine in association with a time when his disciples are with him in immortal life.


**Sources for quotes:**
1. Guerber, H A - *'Myths and Legends of Greece and Rome'*. Original source - Virgil - Warton (trans.)

## Hymn to Dionysus

Dionysus, Dionysus,
draw near to us,
flow into us,
join our frenzied dance.
Stain our lips scarlet,
fill us with the blood-red juice
of the slaughtered vine.
Lord, inspire us,
let your spirit drive us,
wild and wilder.
Pour into us,
enter us,
throb in our pulse,
burn hotter than fire.
On, on and on,
become nothing,
become one,
mad with desire,
spinning, singing, screaming,
in the sacrifice of self.

# Autumn Equinox Rite

Collect seasonal fruits and flowers, and place them on a russet cloth on a table or on the ground. Preferably pick a bunch of grapes from a home-grown vine, giving thanks as you do so, otherwise you will need to buy them. Also, have ready a chalice or glass of red wine.

If you wish, cast a sacred circle around your place of working and request the blessings of the elemental powers in the quarters.

Then, standing in front of the decorated altar, speak these or similar words:

*'The buds of spring have blossomed and borne fruit, and the fruit has been gathered. Now the year draws gently to its rest like the setting sun that glows red over the western ocean.*

*'The Autumn Equinox is a feast of thanksgiving. Great Mother of Life (Rhiannon/Demeter/Isis........), I give thanks for the earth's fruit and for the fruit of experience gained throughout the waxing season. Joyful or sad, easy or challenging, all experiences are gifts of learning. Each brings its own lesson like the light and dark halves of the year. This time marks the completion of the year's harvest, both inner and outer.'*

Hold your wand/forefinger over the bunch of grapes, then over the chalice of wine as you request the Great Mother's blessing on them.

Eat a few grapes and meditate on your own personal harvest which is the result of all that has happened over the past year.

*'But the harvest is not the end, for the grape is transmuted into the flowing wine, as experience is transmuted into wisdom.'* **Drink some of the wine and say:** *'I give thanks for the wine of wisdom.'*

Meditate again, on this and on how releasing that which is outworn but nevertheless clung to for a sense of security, can bring positive change, a chance to move forward.

Face west, the quarter of the Autumn Equinox and say:

*'In the west lies deep love and understanding. Great Mother, may I be blessed with joyous life, wisdom, inspiration and love. So that I may share these blessings in the world.'*

Finally, give thanks and unwind the circle. Leave the remainder of the grapes outside and sprinkle the wine on the earth as an offering.

The branches of a dead tree appear stark against the skyline, above a trunk swathed in deep green foliage.


Ivy, Gort, Eiddew,
evergreen garland,
King Wren's sacred sanctuary.
Follower of the spiral path,
I come in peace and in search of wisdom.
My greetings and blessings to you and all your kin.
Is it your wish to share your knowledge and energy with me?

# Ivy

The common ivy (*Hedera helix*) is an evergreen climber that can attach itself to tree trunks, rocks and walls by sending out root-like fibres known as haustoria. If these come into contact with soil or living matter such as a tree, the ivy will absorb nourishment and sap the tree's strength.

Ivy takes on a bushy character once it reaches the top of its climbing surface, when the upper leaves become pale green and oval, unlike the dark five-lobed leaves lower down. Only then does it produce its small green flowers, which appear between September and December as most vegetation is dying back for the year. In late winter/early spring green berries develop, turning matt black as they ripen, providing valuable out of season food for birds.

According to the Irish Brehon Law, ivy is classed as a Bramble, carrying the least severe penalty for unlawful felling. Yet despite its relatively low staus, it was used to crown the winners of early Welsh Eisteddfodau. The classical Greeks also honoured poets by crowning them with ivy.

Because of its evergreen leaves, ivy became a symbol of fidelity presented to newly-wed couples by the priests of ancient Greece. And ivy boughs adorned the altars dedicated to Hymen, god of marriage and attendant to Venus, goddess of love.

Like the vine, ivy is sacred to the Greek Dionysus and his Roman counterpart Bacchus, associated with drunkenness and wild revelry but later worshipped within the mystery cults, where his death and resurrection were symbolized by the transmutation of grapes into wine. In classical art Dionysus/ Bacchus is depicted as a youth crowned with ivy or vine leaves and holding an ivy bound wand known as the thyrsus. His festival took place in October, the season of the ivy's flowering as well as of the grape harvest and, like the god himself, Bacchanalian revellers wore ivy crowns and carried branches of fir entwined with ivy. Both vine and ivy were linked with death and resurrection, the ivy symbolizing eternal life through its evergreen leaves, winter flowers and spiral growth, reminiscent of the continually spiralling pattern of life, death and rebirth. It is thought that the followers of Dionysus/Bacchus induced a state of frenzy by chewing ivy leaves, combined with other intoxicants such as ivy liquor or ale brewed from the sap of the silver fir. They may also have ingested the fly agaric toadstool (*amanita muscaria*), its stimulant properties providing the formidable strength to tear victims limb from limb as described in the tales of Pentheus and Orpheus (see Vine chapter).

The ivy-bound fir boughs carried by revellers were sacred not only to Dionysus but to Ariadne. Originally a Cretan goddess worshipped with orgiastic rites involving the sacrifice of male victims, she is best known from the myth of Theseus, in which she appears as a mortal princess, daughter of King Minos of Crete. Each year he demands a sacrifice of seven Athenian youths and seven maidens to feed the Minotaur, a bull-headed monster held at the centre of a labyrinth designed by the master architect Daedalus. When Theseus, prince of Athens, offers himself amongst the victims in the hope of killing the Minotaur, Ariadne takes pity on them and gives him a sword and a ball of twine. He unravels this as he enters the labyrinth, enabling him to find his way out after slaying the monster. The convoluted turns of the labyrinth, and the spiral growth of the ivy, can be seen as representing the inner journey: the path of initiation where personal demons are faced and conquered, and where symbolic rebirth occurs as the hero emerges, victorious, into the light.

According to Roman mythology Bacchus was the son of the great father god Jupiter and a mortal mother, Semele. Interestingly, the Flamen Dialis, high priest of Jupiter in Rome, who was thought to embody the god's spirit, was proscribed from having any contact with the two plants associated with his son. It was taboo for him to touch ivy or even mention its name, or to walk under a vine.

As with Dionysus/Bacchus, ivy and vine were sacred to Osiris, Egyptian god of fertility, the Underworld and resurrection. In wall paintings and papyri his face is often painted green to denote lush growth, linking him with the evergreen ivy. It was also sacred to the Phrygian Attis, god of death and rebirth, associated with the cycles of nature and agriculture, whose castrated priests bore ivy-leaf tattoos.

The link between ivy and vine continues to be found as late as Medieval England, when taverns were recognized by the sign of the ivy bush and wine goblets were sometimes carved from ivy wood, though, ironically, wearing a wreath of ivy leaves or taking an infusion of them in wine was thought to prevent intoxication.

According to rural folk custom in some parts of England, ivy was used to bind the last sheaf cut in a parish, known as the Harvest May, Harvest Bride or Ivy Girl. This was then presented to the farmer who had finished reaping his fields last, and was thought to bring bad luck until the next harvest. The last sheaf, whether from an individual farm or an entire parish, embodied the corn spirit, originally an aspect of the Pagan mother goddess or of her sacrificed son, while ivy symbolized death and rebirth. Usually, the corn dolly made from the last sheaf was honoured, and sown with the following year's crop so the spirit would live on. But in early Pagan societies the reaper who cut it, and who was believed to have killed the corn spirit, would himself have been killed as a sacrifice to ensure its rebirth.

Though ivy was initially banned from churches at Christmas because of its Pagan associations, it played a part in later Yuletide traditions such as the festive battles between Holly Boys and Ivy Girls (see Holly chapter). Mythologically, it is linked with the gold crest wren, Saturn's totem bird, which represents the spirit of the waning year. Known to the early Greeks and Romans as 'Little King', the wren was said to take sanctuary in an ivy bush before being killed to make way for the spirit of the waxing year, an event re-enacted around Christmas from classical times until the present day in the ceremony of killing the wren (see under Holly for further detail).

Twisting and entwining as it grows, ivy symbolically weaves together the eternal cycle of birth, death and rebirth. Evergreen, ever living, representing the feminine in nature, it is Ariadne's thread that guides the initiate through the labyrinth of existence.

Ivy is my nature,
my spirit,
ivy at the foot
of the seventh stone.


Green and glossy,
dappled softly in sun and shade.
Warm sun, warm stone.
Dewdrops my diamond rings,
gossamer my veil,
hand in hand with my sisters,
shod in moss, I dance.


Oak and beech,
the pillars of my hall,
its carpet, golden leaves.
My gown is emerald.
Red sun, cold stone.


Whisper of wind,
hum of granite.
Round.......round the circle.
Crackling laughter of twigs,
sleepy breath of earth,
filling us all.
Dreaming, swaying, waiting.
Delicate guardians:
leaf to stem, stem to root, root to leaf.

# Travelling the Labyrinth

At the centre of the '*Wood Wisdom*' ivy card is an image of the labyrinth that can be seen engraved on a rock in Rocky Valley, near Tintagel, Cornwall, identical in design to those that appear on coins from Knossos, Crete, dating from the first-millennium BC.

The words maze and labyrinth are often used interchangeably, though the Cretan design is a true labyrinth, with its single convoluted path to the centre, whereas examples with blind ends and several choices of pathway are more accurately described as mazes. Both forms, whether simple or intricate, ultimately derive from the spiral that occurs so frequently in the natural world, as in the growth pattern of the ivy.

Labyrinths, mazes and spiral patterns can all be found in the British Isles, some dating from prehistoric times, some relatively recent; some clearly constructed for sacred purposes, others for recreation. Most examples are cut in turf, often near pre-historic sites, giving a clue as to their ancient origins, and though the majority are in fact of unicursal design, ie. with one single path to the centre, they are popularly known as mazes rather than labyrinths.

Newgrange Neolithic passage grave in County Meath, Ireland, displays notable carvings of spiral design, almost certainly related to death and rebirth or initiation. Turf mazes or labyrinths in England include: Saffron Walden, Essex; Wing, Leicestershire; Julian's Bower, Alkborough, South Humberside; St. Catherine's Hill Maze, Winchester; Breamore Mizmaze, Hants; and Dalby, Yorkshire. The intricate patterns of Celtic knotwork, as seen on early Christian stone crosses and illuminated manuscripts, are similar in concept to the labyrinth and can he used for the same purposes.

To travel inwards to the centre of the spiral/labyrinth is to enter an altered state of consciousness, or the Under/Otherworld, and to undergo the symbolic death of initiation, while to move outwards again represents rebirth and enlightenment after the transformative experience of entering a place of inner challenge. In ancient Celtic belief the abode of the blessed dead was known as Spiral Castle, a name that occurs in bardic poetry and which is connected with Caer Arianrhod, the Corona Borealis - Ariadne's crown of stars, according to Greek myth.

Christianity also uses the image of the labyrinth to symbolize entry into another realm, with heaven represented by the centre. Carvings of labyrinths are sometimes found in old churches, and a magnificent example of a tiled labyrinth, 40 foot across, can be seen on the floor of Chartres Cathedral in France.

The original purpose of the labyrinths still in existence, and the many that have been destroyed, could have involved more than symbolic death and rebirth as a Czech inventor, Robert Pavlita, proved that visually tracing a pattern similar to a figure eight was able to generate energy. In Paganism, ancient and modern, circle and spiral dancing is used to raise power for magical ends. Spirals and labyrinths may, therefore, have provided a means of creating energy, and of distributing it across the land or into a sacred artefact, through a form of science long since lost to us.

There are seven circuits to the classic Cretan style labyrinth depicted on the ivy card, leading to an eighth loop at the centre, the point of complete darkness and surrender before emergence to rebirth. Because seven is a highly symbolic number, for example the seven ancient planets, the seven notes in a musical octave, the seven chakras and the seven colours of the rainbow, travelling the labyrinth on the sevenfold path enables the seeker to resonate with a set of correspondences for each circuit. And, as you turn clockwise, then anticlockwise, crossing from one side of the labyrinth to the other, personal harmony is achieved between the forces of creation/destruction, light/dark, yin/yang etc., and the chakras are balanced. The labyrinthine journey leads to inner peace and profound insight, new awareness and transformation, though this will only happen through one-pointed focus and deep concentration.

A large labyrinth/maze can be walked or danced, while a small one can be traced with a finger and/or followed with the eye, alternatively a spiral can be visualized and explored on the inner planes.

Outside, the labyrinth can be drawn with chalk, laid out with small stones, or scratched in the sand on a beach. Indoors, it can be marked out with tape. It looks complicated but is surprisingly simple to draw once you know the basic pattern, as is the triple spiral found on the curbstones at Newgrange.

Cretan Labyrinth:
1. Draw a cross, with a curved line in each segment:

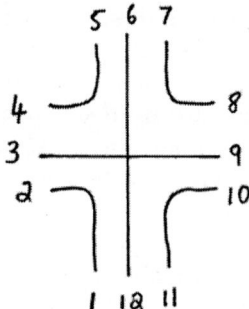

2. Join 1 to 12; 3 to 10; 4 to 9; 6 to 7; extend 2 clockwise curving around the course of the 3 to 10 line, stopping just short of 11; extend 5 to curve above the 6 to 7 line, stopping just short of 8; extend 8 in another curve directly above the 5 line, stopping just short of 4; extend 11 anti-clockwise around

the 2 line, stopping just short of 1, and so the labyrinth is complete.

**Triple spiral:**
Draw a spiralling S-shape leaving space between the curves.

Draw a second spiralling S-shape nestling into this space.

Draw a third spiral to the left of the double spiral, again leaving space between the curves, and add a second spiral within the gaps.

Extend the outer ends of this single interlinked spiral, one clockwise, one anti-clockwise to surround the double spiral to the right.

Long, tapering leaves are reflected in a shallow swamp, whispering as a breeze skims across the waters:

Reed, Ngetal, Cawnen,
straight as a shaft of sunlight,
spanning earth, water and air.
Piper of Pan's soft music,
I come in peace and in search of wisdom.
My greetings and blessings to you and all your kin.
Is it your wish to share your knowledge and energy with me?

# Reed

The reed (*Phragmites communis*) is a form of tall grass which grows in marshy areas or at the margins of rivers and lakes. It has long leaves, up to an inch wide, and straight stalks topped with feathery seed heads. Reeds are cut in November to be used for roof thatch, while rushes and sedges, which share the same habitat and are broadly similar in appearance, are used for weaving chair seats, baskets and other craft items.

The Medieval Irish Brehon Law tree classification does not include reed in any of its four categories, indicating that there were no restrictions on cutting it.

As the symbolism of the ivy results from its spiral growth pattern, so the symbolism of the reed is largely associated with its straightness. Because of this it came to be linked with the rays of the sun, and arrows, also representative of the sun's rays, were often made from reed.

In Dynastic Egypt the Pharaoh, living embodiment of the sun god Ra, carried a reed sceptre, and throughout the eastern Mediterranean the reed was a royal plant, almost certainly due to its solar connections and its form, the concept of good rulership being linked with straightness - straight forward, direct and strong. This widespread association is found etymologically in the English word ruler: a tool for creating a straight line, or a monarch, one who lays down rules that must be followed, not deviating from the straight and narrow. The ancient Egyptian '*Book of the Dead*' describes the Otherworld as the Field of Reeds, Sekhet-Aaru, a paradise equivalent to the Greek Elysian Fields, which the deceased must make his or her way to, overcoming many dangers. Once in the Field of Reeds, the soul was thought to need a boat to negotiate the canals and streams, so in the belief that the image of an object equalled its actuality in the Afterworld, a boat would be depicted on the funerary papyrus placed with the sarcophagus.

In Greek myth the reed is central to the tale of Syrinx, a nymph desired by Pan, god of the wild. Once, as Pan pursued her, she prayed to Gaia (or in other versions to her father, the river-god Ladon) for protection, and in answer to her plea was transformed into a reed (clump of reeds). Lonely and frustrated at his loss, Pan let out a desolate sigh, a sound made ever since by the wind rustling through a reed bed. Still thinking about Syrinx, he then cut seven pieces of reed, each a fraction longer than the last, and bound them together, forming a pipe which he named after her. In classical art he is usually depicted holding the syrinx, which is said to enchant anyone who hears it being played.

Reeds are frequently used as, and in, wind instruments, for example inside the mouthpiece of a clarinet, and in the past formed the pipes of Irish and Scottish bagpipes, mythologically invented in the world of faery. Because of their hollow centre and gift of music, reeds are associated with the element air, which in turn is linked to the breath of life and the unseen spirit that flows through each living thing.

**Reflection**

Somewhere the sound of pipes,
or just the faintest breath of wind
visiting............


..........a place of pools and rhynes,
neither land nor sea,
a place between worlds,
of vast empty skies,
of waters, smooth as glass.


.........a time of silent dreams,
neither night nor day,
a dusky pink hour
when reed stalks pierce the mist,
dark against the sky above
and the sky below.


.........a faery realm, reflecting ours
or in ours reflected,
the veil rippling as
a teal takes wing
in soul flight
to a land below the waters,
carrying its message
from sky to sky.


.........a marshy wilderness
where the poised heron fishes,
plunging its mirrored beak
into this world to catch
a glimpse of mortality.

Slowly, slowly
the breeze rises,
raking up the pools.
And the reeds sigh in grief
for a sunken world
that is no more.

# The Homeless Spirits

It was towards the end of the holidays - soon Doug's two grandchildren would be back at school, cooped up in a stuffy classroom, so he had brought them out to the river where the late summer sun glimmered on the water and a fresh breeze sighed through the reeds that lined the banks. After sharing a picnic, they sat quietly on the grass as he waited to show them a mallard or moorhen, birds that were once common here, but there was no sign of life, and in places he began to notice a dirty skum lurking at the water's edge. When he looked more closely he also realized that many of the reeds were dead or dying, their leaves twisted and brown.

Before long Dan and Lucy had had enough of sitting still, searching for something that did not seem likely to appear. As he watched them run along the rough path, Doug shouted after them,

'Stay within sight and don't touch the water, it's polluted.'

'OK,' ten year-old Lucy called back over her shoulder, obviously not bothered by the idea - something children these days were used to, he supposed.

Still keeping an eye on them, Doug found a part of his mind drifting back to when he was their age, over sixty years ago. He knew he would have been shocked if anyone had told him to keep clear of the water. He and his mate Bert spent every weekend of the summer here, sometimes just the two of them, sometimes with a gang of friends and younger brothers who had tagged along. Always unsupervised by adults - that was another thing that had changed.

He could see Bert now, red hair and freckles, thigh deep in the river beside him, net in one hand, jar of stickle-backs in the other. The water was cold on his own legs as he waded out as far as he dared, peering down and down, right down to the stones and weeds on the river bed. Some were russet, some brown, others various shades of green, all healthy and abundant, the home of tiny water snails.

He straightened up and looked across to the far bank where a family of swans were nesting amongst the reeds, and the air was alive with the song of birds and the hum of insects. Then, seeing that Bert was distracted, he scooped up a handful of chill water, aiming it at the back of his neck.

'I'll have you Dougie Wright.......I'll have you.'

Throwing his net onto the bank, Bert put all his energy into getting revenge until both boys were breathless with laughter and drenched to the skin. The only thing they were worried about was what their mothers would say. Water was just water: clean, safe and fun.

When they had had enough they scrambled out, adding mud to the water on their clothes, and paused to count who had caught the most stickle-backs - the loser had sworn to buy the victor a bag of ha'penny gob-stoppers. But, before the counting was finished, Doug felt a sudden chill, no doubt because of his damp clothes. He blinked.

Dan and Lucy were still playing in a meadow nearby, though the sun had been swallowed by a black cloud which had built up from nothing within minutes, and already there were spots of rain. Doug smiled to himself at the thought of how he would get in trouble with his daughter if he brought the children back soaking, just as he had once faced his mother's anger. A little stiffly, he got to his feet and began to pack up the picnic basket, stopping at intervals to call for Dan and Lucy. They eventually obeyed when a gust of wind whipped across the land with such force that they struggled to keep their balance. Lucy even took her grandad's hand for reassurance as they headed back to his cottage where the children's parents had been having an afternoon to themselves.

Though it was only a short walk, by the time they reached the garden gate rain was lashing into their faces, driven by a wind that became stronger with each gust. Doug noticed a distinct expression of relief on his daughter Sarah's face when they appeared, and guessed she had been looking out for them.

She smiled at Lucy and Dan, faking nonchalance, while their father called out from the sitting room.

'Have a good time?'

Dan glanced eagerly through the open door at the football game on the TV, but Sarah pushed him towards the stairs. 'Go and put on some dry clothes first, then we'll have tea.

'Shame the weather changed.' She moved towards the window, catching her breath as a furious gust brought an apple branch down right outside, and hurled a battery of stones and debris against the glass. 'I've never seen anything like it. Thank God you got back in time.' 'It did come on suddenly, but we've had a few violent storms recently, just local.........'

He was interrupted by Lucy, who came flying down the stairs to her mother, a blend of fear and excitement in her voice.

'The wind's alive, mum. It's throwing stones at the cottage. It won't blow away will it? Like the house in 'The Wizard of Oz'?

Sarah laughed, a trifle nervously. A second later the television went off and they were plunged into stormy half-light.

Doug himself was now standing by the window, vaguely aware of his son-in-law's curses and Dan's moans that they would miss the match, their voices mingling with Lucy's cries and Sarah complaining that now she could not use the kettle. Through the driving rain, he stared out across the meadow towards the river, where he could just see the tallest of the reeds slashing beneath mauve storm clouds. He was about to turn away when he stared again, wondering if he was on the verge of senility. He seemed to be watching sinuous forms, like curls of smoke or ghostly snakes, writhing upward from the reeds themselves, building the cloud into an ever thicker mass, whipping the wind into a frenzy of anger, spinning round and round, rising from river to sky.

Then, what he had seen earlier - the brown skummy water, the brown withered reeds - flashed into his mind, followed by an image of the place as it had been in his childhood - vegetation rich and green, filled with the spirit of life that was now being driven out by a toxic residue from field and factory. Perhaps he was over-tired from entertaining the children, perhaps it was grief over the lost simplicity of his youth playing tricks with his imagination, but the life of the river was dying, there was no ignoring that.

A squat tree with dark thorny branches grows at the side of a lonely track, its shadow elongated by the mid-winter sunlight.

Blackthorn, Straif, Draenen ddu,
blossom white as frost,
flowering when the earth is cold.
Giver of bitter blue fruit,
I come in peace and in search of wisdom.
My greetings and blessings to you and all your kin.
Is it your wish to share your knowledge and energy with me?

# Blackthorn

The blackthorn (*Prunus spinosa*) is native to the British Isles and able to survive on most soils. It can reach the height of a small tree, up to 4m, but is more commonly found amongst other hedgerow shrubs or forming a dense thicket. Though it usually produces its haze of small white blossoms around March/April, the blackthorn sometimes flowers in the depths of winter, even during periods of frost and snow. This often happens after a mild spell or 'false spring' and is known as a 'blackthorn winter' or 'the blackthorn hatch'.

From late August the blue-black fruit or sloes, with their waxy purple bloom, are visible on the branches, ripening only after the first frosts. All cultivated damson and plum varieties originally derive from the wild blackthorn though, unlike the sweet juicy fruit of domesticated trees, sloes have an extrem-ely bitter taste. They can be used for sloe gin - an almond scented liquor which is made by filling half a bottle with pricked sloes, adding several spoonfuls of sugar and topping up with gin. The mixture is then shaken vigorously and left to mature for up to a year.

The Medieval Irish Brehon Law classifies blackthorn as a Shrub, a lower status tree, and in folk belief it has come to be regarded as malevolent because of its dark colour and vicious thorns, and because its fruit ripens after Samhain, the Celtic feast of the dead; also because of its association with the occult, extended into anti-Pagan propaganda.

Odin/Woden, northern god of the dead, war and runic wisdom carried a blackthorn staff when he entered the realm of humankind, shrouded in a grey cloak and accompanied by two ravens and a wolf. He may have been a deified tribal shaman, who had gained his gifts through initiatory ordeal and descent to the Underworld. Mortal shamans, too, were once identified by the blackthorn staff they carried - both as a symbol of their vocation and as a tool for wielding power.

The rune Thurisaz (Elder Futhark), Thorn (Anglo-Saxon Futhorc) has several possible interpretations, including giant and demon, while the *'Old English Rune Poem'* (c. 9th century AD) describes it as sharp, cruel and harmful. The late twelfth century *'Old Norwegian Rune Rhyme'* states that Thurs causes women to become ill and brings misfortune.

Considering the symbolism, it is most likely that the species of thorn associated with this powerful rune was the blackthorn. When used magically, Thurisaz/Thorn was believed to alter the meaning of succeeding runes if repeated three times and to be capable of evoking Underworld demons.

Reminiscent of 'The Old Norwegian Rune Rhyme', according to a Devon belief still held in the early twentieth century a witch's 'black rod', which doubled as a walking stick, could cause miscarriage. Two hundred years earlier, the seventeenth century Scottish witch Major Weir was said to have used his blackthorn staff as a magical weapon, the reason why it accompanied him into the flames when he was burnt at the stake in 1670. Blackthorn spikes were also employed by sorcerers to prick the waxen image of an intended victim.

Because of its hardness, blackthorn wood was not only suitable for witches' staffs and mundane walking sticks, but for war clubs, like the Irish club or shillelagh. In Latin blackthorn is 'bellicum', etymologically associating it with aggression, either physical or astral; and the word 'strife' may well derive from *'Straif'* through the old Northern French *'estrif'*, which in turn derives from the Breton language with its Celtic roots. Another link is found in the etymological connection between the English words 'sloe' and 'slay'.

Though blackthorn staffs often have negative connotations, a rod made from blackthorn is still used by the Usher of the House of Lords in the traditional practice of knocking on the chamber door at the annual opening of Parliament, giving the holder of the post the title 'Blackrod'.

Some areas of the country generally regarded the blackthorn as favourable, using it for blessing rather than cursing, and in Worcestershire the ashes of a blackthorn crown that had been ceremonially burnt were scattered on the fields to promote fertility. In northern England, good fortune was attracted by a wreath of blackthorn and mistletoe hung inside at New Year, while a ball made from its twigs played a part in winter wassailing ceremonies, performed to encourage an abundant crop of cider apples.

According to Christian tradition, Christ's Crown of Thorns was of blackthorn, which supposedly will not grow in the vicinity of hawthorn (whitethorn), symbolic of purification and chastity. With both there is a taboo on bringing the flowering branches inside except for specific seasonal festivals and, like the Glastonbury Holy Thorn, said to have been planted by Joseph of Arimathea (see Hawthorn chapter), blackthorn was thought to blossom on Christmas Day.

Just as the interpretation of a rune or Ogham stave depends on how it falls, the way a sacred tree is regarded varies according to region and era, whether Christian or Pagan - so blackthorn defies judgement in simple dualistic terms.

## Triads

Three clouds of fear:
The tangled thicket in thorny fight.
The winding path, glazed with ice.
The sun's decline, the longest night.


Three rays of hope:
White blossom on the winter thorn.
The pathway straight and clear, though long.
Solstice sunrise, the Mabon reborn.


Three fruits of fulfilment:
Ripe black sloes, with velvet bloom.
A welcome when the journey's done.
The soul's sun bright, eternal noon.

# Winter Meditation

During the depths of winter take a walk down a country lane bordered by hedgerows or in a remote area. Alternatively, perform an inner journey if a physical one is impractical. In either case, look out for a blackthorn bush, identifiable by its bark and the occasional sloe berry that has not been eaten by birds still clinging to the bare branches.

Begin with a suitable greeting then, if you feel welcome, stand in meditation, focusing on the intertwined pattern of branch and thorn, on the tone and texture of the sloes, on the buds waiting to burst into flower (or in flower during a 'blackthorn hatch').

The blackthorn is a tree of opposites, in the whiteness of its blossom and the darkness of its bark, the sharp thorns and the rounded fruit. In a similar way, life is composed of interdependent contrasts, illustrated by the Chinese Yin/Yang symbol with its black and white comma shapes locked together within the circle of completion, a white dot in the black section, a black dot in the white. Male/female, day/night, action/repose, heat/cold, creation/destruction, etc. - both sides of every pair are of equal importance, as one cannot exist without the other and can only be identified by comparison to its opposite, while in each the potential of the other is always present.

The above offers material for meditation, particularly relevant at the season when, in an apparently bleak world, buds are swelling on bare branches and the leaves of bluebells and other bulbs have already pushed through the frozen earth. By contrast, the heat of late summer is a time of death in life: the buds have all flowered and begun to fruit, the growth energy spent as plants and trees wind down towards winter.

After a while leave the blackthorn and find other examples of life in death, blending what is visible around you with meditation. When you are ready, give thanks to the blackthorn and the spirits of nature you have worked with, whether on both the outer and inner planes or only on the inner, and return to ordinary consciousness.

Amongst the fruits and flowers of early autumn, a crooked tree wears its berries like purple beads.


Elder, Ruis, Ysgawen,
Ceridwen's companion,
shadowy, bent and bowed.
Witch-tree of the waning year,
I come in peace and in search of wisdom.
My greetings and blessings to you and all your kin.
Is it your wish to share your knowledge and energy with me?

# Elder

The elder (*Sambucus nigra*) is a hardy and extremely fast-growing shrub, found throughout Europe except in the far north. Readily taking root in cracked paths or on rough ground, it usually occurs as a bush with spreading branches, though it can form a small tree of up to 10m in height. The serated leaves are either narrow or rounded and the bark deeply ridged, identifiable by small dark 'warts'.

In June the elder produces umbrella-shaped clusters of tiny white flowers with a sharp scent, often used for making elderflower cordial. The berries are green at first and become purplish-black when ripe in late August or September, their darkness contrasting with bright red stalks. Like the flowers they are used in country recipes, such as elderberry wine which alleviates the symptoms of colds, influenza and bronchial infection. The elder blossom, leaves and berries all possess medicinal qualities, recognized for centuries and now proved effective by modern science.

Elder represents the thirteenth letter of the Ogham tree alphabet, and is classified as a Shrub according to the Medieval Irish Brehon Law. Robert Graves' tree calendar allocates it to the lunar month of November/December, a period beginning shortly after Samhain (Hallowe'en) and leading up to the darkest day of the Winter Solstice.

Elder has long been regarded as a tree of death, and flints from Neolithic long-barrows knapped in the form of its leaves indicate that this symbolism already existed at least five thousand years ago. The elder's funerary associations also extend throughout Europe, shown by the Tyrolean custom of trimming an elder tree into the shape of a cross and planting it on a new grave. If it blossomed, it was taken to mean that the soul of the deceased was at peace. In Wales and the Isle of Man a similar custom prevailed, along with the Celtic practice of placing green elder boughs in the grave itself to guard the departed against witchcraft and evil spirits.

Death legends linked with the elder include a belief that the archer who slew King William Rufus in the New Forest was standing beneath an elder tree when he fired the fatal arrow. The cross of the crucifixion is said to have been made from elder wood, though this is not specified in the Bible, and since the Middle Ages it has been falsely thought that Judas hanged himself from an elder tree - according to the biblical account of his death (Acts ch.1, v.18) he simply falls, causing him to 'burst asunder in the midst'. The tale of his suicide occurs in, or possibly originates from, William Langland's *'Vision of Piers Plowman'*, written in the mid-fourteenth century:

> *'Judas he japed with Jewen silver*
> *And sithen an eller hanged hymselve.'*

The heady scent of an elder thicket was once said to cause mortal sickness, but according to the ancient Danes anyone who stood under an elder on Midsummer's Eve would see the king of the faeries and his retinue pass by. This is reminiscent of the ballad of Thomas the Rhymer (Thomas of Erceldoune, c.1220-97), who encountered the Queen of Faerie whilst sitting beneath what is described as the 'Eildon Tree'. He then accompanied her into the Otherworld for seven years, becoming her lover and obtaining the gift of prophecy. Though not identified as a particular species, the name 'Eildon Tree' closely resembles several words for elder used in the past, such as 'ellan' and the Medieval 'hylantree'; it is also similar to the Anglo-Saxon *'eldrum'* and Low Saxon *'elhorn'*.

In northern Europe, especially in Denmark, the elder was thought to be the dwelling place of a dryad spirit known as the Elder Tree Mother, whose permission was required before pruning or felling the tree. If elder timber was made into furniture she would remain with it, haunting the house where the furniture was taken, nor should a child be placed in a cradle made of elder wood in case s/he pined away, or was molested either by faeries or by the Elder Tree Mother herself.

According to traditional belief, witches were capable of shape-shifting into the form of an elder, an idea perhaps triggered by its rapid growth or because people reputed to be witches were usually skilled herbalists, associated with administering elder for its medicinal properties. Another reason may have been that in Ireland elder wood was used for witches' besom handles.

Often in folklore, the same thing that was thought to attract harm was also thought to repel it. Therefore, in order to protect the home from evil, elder leaves were gathered on May Eve and fixed above doors and windows. Elder growing close to houses acted in a similar way, as well as offering protection against lightning, as the tree was supposedly never struck.

The word elder derives from the Anglo-Saxon word *'ëld'* - 'fire', recalling an ancient practice of blowing through the hollow stems to fan embers into flame. Yet the elder itself is notoriously bad for firewood, and burning its logs was said to invite the devil into the house.

In the lore of the elder, we see how a set of beliefs and taboos surrounding a tree sacred to Pagan goddesses of death and magic degenerated into rural superstition. But despite negative associations, the elder has always been valued for culinary and healing purposes, and for its beauty when in flower.

**Sources for quotes:**
Quoted in - Grieve, M - *'A Modern Herbal'*.

Her ways are solitary:
far from human strife,
she stands alone,
a haunted form seen
by the half-lit path
on autumn nights.

Freckled limbs, strong and lithe,
in a soft green gown
and creamy blossom crown,
she welcomes spring,
as she welcomes all
who come seeking her.

To sleep beside her
is to dream strange dreams
on balmy scented evenings,
drifting through the open door
to a world of faery feasts.

Her body carries
a thousand remedies.
She has power to banish sickness
with the gifts from her magic store.
And she'll give wine by the jarful
beneath the Harvest Moon,
celebrating the season's turn,
though she knows full well
that soon her own beauty
too will turn and wane.

And once again she is shunned.
Who dares approach
the stark skeleton
stripped of her finery?
With nothing more to give,
she watches over the moment
when day greets the longest winter night.

# Samhain Rite

Samhain was the ancient Celtic new year's eve and feast of the dead, when the spirits of those who had crossed the threshold were welcomed back amongst their loved ones. According to Robert Graves' tree calendar, the Yew is allocated to Samhain itself, however, the elder, which shares much of its funerary symbolism, is equally relevant to this festival.

The deities worked with in the following rite are Cerridwen: goddess of wisdom, magic and transformation - through death/rebirth or initiation - and also of fertility/plenty; and Gwyn ap Nudd: Brythonic lord of the dead and master of the wild hunt, whose realm is said to be reached through Glastonbury Tor.

The elder will already have shed its leaves by the end of October, though a few bare branches can be cut for decorating the altar, as always, giving honour and asking permission. Alternatively, place the 'Wood Wisdom' elder card and/or a drawing of the tree on your altar, along with seasonal symbols, a black and a white candle and a large ashtray or fire resistant container. You will also need a pen and paper - no larger than 8 x 12cm or it will create too much of a blaze when burnt. And a chalice of red wine and a dish of apple and nuts should be placed in readiness.

Light the black candle and any others you are using for illumination, but not the white at this stage. Cast a circle around your place of working with the words:

'I cast this circle to be a sacred space, a place of truth and light, and a barrier against all harm.'

Then, if you wish, request the guardianship of the elemental powers before saying:

'Lady Cerridwen, Lord Gwyn, I give you honour and ask your blessings upon my rite.

'Between earth and sky I stand in this circle to mark the closing of the old year and the opening of the new: a time when the veil between worlds is thin and the spirits of those who have gone to the Isles of the Blest walk again with the living.'

Take as long as you need to think about any fears, grievances, bad habits etc. that you want to free yourself from. Write them down, fold the paper and say:

> *'In each end, a new start.*
> *As the snake sloughs its skin,*
> *as the cocoon bursts,*
> *as the growing shoot breaks*
> *shell and husk,*
> *these things I release with the old year: ............'*

Still speaking, light the paper from the black candle, place it in the fireproof container and allow it to burn. Only when it is reduced to ashes should you light the white candle, saying:

*'From the depths of the cauldron*
*wisdom is won.*
*From the womb the infant is born.*
*From the darkest of nights, a new dawn.*
*In the black earth*
*the seed is sown*
*and springs forth.*

*These things I wish to be and achieve in the coming year* (list them aloud). *May this flame be a symbol of bright beginnings.'*

Pause to reflect on the resolutions you have just made, visualizing them coming to fruition. Then face the altar/table on which the dish and chalice have been placed, requesting that the feast be blessed by Cerridwen.

When this is done, raise the chalice towards the west.

*'To the those who now dwell in the Summerlands. I remember and honour the ancestors: my own kin and my ancestors in spirit. I bid you welcome, all who come in peace and good will.'*

Take a few sips before raising the plate of apple and nuts:

*'I share this feast with those who have returned over the threshold to be with me for this one night of Samhain.'*

Eat a little (leaving enough to make an offering later) as you sense the closeness of all whom you have invited, extending warmth and blessings towards them. You will probably then wish to sit in meditation and remembrance for a while.

When you feel ready, stand and raise the chalice for a second time with the words:

*'To the new year.'*

Take a few sips, again leaving some, put the wine aside and turn to the altar:

*'Lady Cerridwen, Lord Gwyn, I thank you for your blessings and for the lessons you teach, for though they are often harsh they bring wisdom and understanding. Blessings and farewell to all who have joined me this night, may you return to your realm in peace and joy.'*

If it can be done without causing a fire hazard, leave the white candle alight until it burns away to nothing, perhaps placing it outside - a symbol of hope during a time of darkness and chaos, a time when worlds mingle, and when the old year is in the process of breaking down with the energies of the new one not yet stabilized.

Finally, give thanks to the elemental powers, unwind the circle, and make an offering to the ancestors by leaving the remainder of the wine, apple and nuts in the garden or out in the wild.

Gusts of wind sprinkle snow from the branches of a fir that stands in the darkest depths of the forest.

Fir, Ailm, Ffynidwydden,
noble prince of the north,
Midwinter's joy.
Spirit of life, ever green,
I come in peace and in search of wisdom.
My greetings and blessings to you and all your kin.
Is it your wish to share your knowledge and energy with me?

# Silver Fir

The common silver fir (*Abies alba*) can reach a height of 50m, and has a narrow ragged outline. On young trees the bark is smooth and silvery, though as they mature it becomes brown and cracked. The flat needle-leaves, which are green-blue in colour, are distinguished by a marked central ridge and white strips on the underside. Cylindrical female cones form only on the upper branches, while the male flowers occur at all levels. Though it has been planted for timber, the species is not native to Britain and originates in the mountainous regions of central Europe, where it grows in dense forests.

I have dealt with the natural history of the silver fir, but its mythic associations can be applied to any variety of fir. The position of first vowel in the Ogham alphabet is also sometimes attributed to pine, and there is a cross-over between the symbolism of the two trees. Pine, not fir, features in the Irish Brehon Law as a Chieftain tree, for 'being in the puncheon'.

Mythologically, fir is the tree of birth, and in ancient Greece was sacred to Artemis, goddess of the moon and of childbirth. In Old Irish '*Ailm*' meant fir and palm - the birth tree of the Middle East.

Both fir and pine cones have phallic/fertility associations, as shown by the ivy-bound rods tipped with a pine cone that were carried by the ecstatic worshippers of Dionysus/Bacchus. The Phrygian Attis shared this connection with the pine, and according to legend the goddess Cybele transformed him into a pine after he had been fatally wounded by a boar or, in other versions, had emasculated himself beneath a pine tree. The pine was representative of eternal life, of death and rebirth, though in contrast to the fir, associated with the rebirth of the sun at the Winter Solstice, the pine was linked to the rebirth of the vegetation god in Mediterranean and Middle Eastern New Year rites, which were celebrated at the Spring Equinox.

In the tree calendar, the silver fir can be placed either on

the Winter Solstice itself, the shortest day when the sun's power is no longer on the decline, or on the following day, when the light is again waxing.

During Pagan Winter Solstice rites the fir's evergreen boughs may well have been brought into homes and temples along with holly, ivy, bay and mistletoe, and its symbolic descendent, the Christmas Tree, now usually a Norwegian spruce, still represents birth. The Bible does not say in what month Jesus was born, so the early Christian church chose Midwinter to mark the incarnation of the Christ-child, to coincide with existing Pagan celebrations and assist conversion to the new faith. Several ancient deities, for example the Persian Mithras and the Egyptian Horus, share the same birth-date. Though Christmas Day occurs four days after the Solstice itself, like the Christians after them this is when Pagans would have rejoiced, as by this time it was clear to all, without the aid of astronomical equipment, that the hours of daylight were increasing - the son of the great mother goddess had been reborn.

Bringing a small fir tree inside to celebrate Christmas has its origins in Germany, though exactly when the practice began is unknown. According to legend, Martin Luther was inspired by the sight of the stars shining between the branches of a fir and suggested the idea of a candle-lit tree as a symbol of Christ's birth from the starry heavens. The 'invention' of the Christmas Tree has also been attributed to St Maternus (fourth century) and St Boniface (eighth century): it is said that after he felled a sacred oak on Christmas Eve, a fir sapling sprouted in its place.

The first account of the familiar Christmas Tree, written in Strasburg in 1605, describes people setting up fir trees indoors and decorating them with paper roses, apples, wafers, gold-foil and sweets, a custom that probably stemmed from the ancient Pagan practice of tying rags to sacred trees.

Prince Albert is generally believed to have introduced the Christmas Tree to England in 1841, when a candle-lit fir at Windsor Castle attracted attention, but before this date

German settlers were already following their native custom in various parts of England. By 1870 the new idea had taken hold, and fir trees began to replace the traditional Kissing Bough: a decorated evergreen garland containing mistletoe, which was suspended from the ceiling and acted as a focus for seasonal celebrations.

Even more than mistletoe, fir and spruce have carried the tradition of sacred trees into the modern world. Relevant to both Christians and neo-Pagans, they also hold subliminal power in houses where there is no outward spirituality.

**Sources for quotes:**
1. Commissioners for Publishing the Ancient Laws and Institutes of Ireland - *'Ancient Laws of Ireland, Vol IV'*.

Midwinter at noon,
snow began to fall,
fine as lightest goose down
on silver-green boughs
and nut-brown cones.
The tangled forest floor
and sloping thatch
of house and barn became
smooth-iced, like a cake.
Men herded flocks to safety
while children ran and played,
shouts crisp and clear,
until, for a moment, the setting sun
poured its red wine
over each frozen bough.
Then lamps were lit,
pools of gold on velvet ground.
Families drew close
beneath woven blankets,
as the forest firs waited
in their blanket of snow.
Lofty, silent guardians
watching through the slow
hours of the longest night,
watching with the scattered stars,
the Dragon, the Hunter and the Plough.
Time's passage was marked
only by the soft rush
of a heavy-laden branch
casting off its burden.
As the darkened village slept
a lone stag stepping through the forest
paused in the clearing
beyond the blacksmith's forge and,
raising his antlered head,
scented snow on the air.

By dawn all trace of his hoof-prints were gone,
their crescent cups filled
by a fresh fall, glistening crisply
in the rays of the infant sun.

# Fools' Paradise

Strings of coloured lights were festooned across the High Street and blazed from the branches of the oversized spruce which dominated the pedestrian precinct. Though the last minute shoppers scarcely noticed as they competed for a rare parking space and glanced continually at their watches, rushing past yet another plastic sign wishing them a 'Merry Christmas'.

Jackie paused to look at a department store window filled with fake snow, and holding her umbrella against the steadily falling rain wondered if she could scrape together enough to buy a pair of brand-name trainers for twelve year old Steven and the computer games that Jo had pleaded for. No - she would have to go for something cheaper or they would never be able to afford next month's mortgage payment. And there was no time to waste in case she needed to shop around for the right bargain. Why had she left it so late, yet again?

In a daze, she turned towards the automatic doors, nearly colliding with a woman half hidden by an armful of carrier bags, who gave her a venomous stare. Inside, her ears were filled with the jingly sounds of *'Winter Wonderland'*. If she heard that tune one more time!!!!!! She tried to shut it out and concentrate on the task in hand. Two more days and it would all be over. Today, the last of the present buying. Tomorrow, enduring the company of David's mother for Christmas dinner. Then back to normal for another year, whatever normal was.

Christmas morning dawned dull and wet. As the children sat under the tree surrounded by crumpled wrapping paper, Jackie noticed that it had already dropped a shower of needles and was looking decidedly past its best. Like all the fancy boxes of bubble bath and talc that no one really wanted, it had one purpose - commerciality. Its life had been created simply so that it could be felled, then stand in someone's living room decorated with baubles and shedding needles onto the carpet.

'Ben said he'd be getting a new computer for Christmas,' Steven's grumpy tones snapped her out of her daydream as he unwrapped the last of his modest presents. Jo at least made some pretence at gratitude, and kissed both her parents on the cheek before disappearing upstairs to play a CD from one of her friends. Only Chloe, at two and a half, was genuinely delighted with her teddy bear. But give it a year, Jackie thought, and she would be demanding over-priced movie-tie-in toys.

Chloe was already less endearing when it came to Christmas dinner, and the second they all sat down she picked up a spoon of cranberry sauce and flicked it onto the pristine white table cloth which had taken half a lifetime to iron.

'Come on, eat properly like a good girl,' Jackie said more calmly than she felt, wiping up the mess with her napkin. But before she had finished, out of the corner of her eye she saw a brussel sprout fly across the table and heard Jo's stifled giggle. Trust Chloe to play up now.

The toddler's triumphant gaze was directed towards David's mother, the audience chosen for her special performance. And this time Jackie could not help catching her mother-in-law's eye.

'You are too indulgent with her. If David ever behaved like that he'd have been sent to his room with no dessert.'

'Mum, she's only two. She's over-excited.'

Jackie took a long mouthful of wine. A niggling comment was how rows always started between David and his mother, rows she always did her best to diffuse or, if that failed, to ignore. But Jo and Steven looked ready to enjoy the confrontation, like an audience anticipating a title fight.

'Would anyone like second helpings?' she asked brightly, and at the same moment was saved by a ring at the doorbell.

It was Meg from down the road, who had a son the same age as Steven. She gave Jackie a perfume-scented hug.

'Merry Christmas.' Then, after a glance over her

shoulder into the dining area. 'Ooooo, I am sorry, haven't you finished eating yet?'

'Um, no. We were rather late starting. The turkey wasn't quite defrosted. But come in and join us if you've got a minute. Have a glass of wine.' Safety in numbers?

'Don't mind if I do. I've left the boys to do the washing up.'

She sat down and offered a toast, then drained the glass she was given in one mouthful. Jackie followed her example before clearing away the dishes.

As she came back from the kitchen she saw Meg eyeing the cards on the mantle with what could only be described as a pitying look.

'We've got just so many cards we've had to string them across all the walls, and in the hall too. We know so many people, there are always dozens of parties this time of year. Of course then there's the problem that I can't wear the same outfit twice, but Nigel has been so generous........Weren't you wearing that dress at Sarah's engagement?'

'Would you like another drink?'

'Wouldn't say no.'

Again Jackie followed Meg's example, downing a whole glass the moment her mother-in-law looked away to begin her Christmas Pudding. She cast a warning glance at Chloe as she put a scoop of ice cream into her bowl, but the child was too fascinated by Meg's diamante earrings to throw any more food, and only managed to spill it down her front.

Not to be outdone by the saintly Nigel, David actually offered to wash up, or rather bribed the older children into doing it, while Jackie said she would walk back with Meg to pick up the presents she had forgotten to bring over. She made her excuses not to stay for a drink, saying it would offend David's mother if she was gone too long, but once Meg had waved her off she changed direction, away from her own house, and turned down a footpath leading between garden fences - the short cut to the park.

During the afternoon the clouds had cleared and now a

187

ruby-red sun hung like a Christmas bauble above the horizon. It was getting chilly and would soon be dark, and the presents in the carrier bag were heavy, but Jackie continued walking. The muzziness in her head soon cleared and she felt suddenly carefree. There were no cars on the usually busy road which she crossed at the end of the footpath, and she had the park entirely to herself. She would make one circuit before going back to the melee. Couldn't be too long or they'd worry, probably inciting a full-blown row.

Halfway round to the play area, Jackie stopped to admire the crimson and coral streaked sky where the sun had just dipped out of sight. Then, silhouetted against the fiery backdrop, she saw a young fir tree, its bark softly silver in the failing light. Strange she had never spotted it before, not in all the times she had taken the children to this corner of the park. As she stared at the branches, decorated by nature with tapering cones, her mind travelled back over past Christmasses, to when Stephen and Jo were laughing toddlers, not difficult individuals on the verge of adolescence. She remembered Chloe's face the first time she held her, tiny and wrinkled but bright as the sun. And when Stephen was born - her first. The wonder and the magic. Too often lately she had allowed herself to forget, not to see it, but that magic was still there, even when he was at his most rebellious, Jo at her most stubborn. After all, the clouds added more beauty to the sunset than a clear sky, and she felt certain that tomorrow would dawn fine. Then she could take Chloe and show her the tree: a real, living Christmas Tree that would still be there when she had children of her own.

Wild and untamed, an area of moorland reaches to the horizon, its bleakness mellowed by a multitude of yellow flowers.

Gorse, Onn, Eithin,
garland of the Flower Bride,
sprinkling your gold across the hillside,
bright as sunlight in spring.
I come in peace and in search of wisdom.
My greetings and blessings to you and all your kin.
Is it your wish to share your knowledge and energy with me?

# Gorse

Gorse (*Ulex Europëus, Linn.*), also known as furze and broom, is an evergreen shrub with dense spiny branches. The bright golden flowers, which have a strong scent, appear from March until August, though an occasional flower may bloom at any time of year. Gorse is common from northern to southern Europe, and is found in open woodland, heath and scrubland, where it thrives on dry soil. Its name describes its habitat, deriving from the Anglo-Saxon word '*gorst*', meaning a wasteland.

In Pliny's writings '*Ulex*' is believed to refer to the gorse, though in later centuries it was defined as a species of broom (*Genista spinosa*) until the Swedish botanist Linnëus redefined it as 'Ulex'. This can cause confusion as it has led to the word 'broom' being used as a synonym for the gorse, though the true broom is another plant altogether (*Cytisus scoparius, Linn.*), known to Pliny and Virgil as 'Genista'. It received its name because its long straight branches were ideal for making brooms - 'scopa' being Latin for a besom. Like the gorse it has golden yellow flowers, and both shrubs produce pods that explode to release their seeds.

The broom was first used as a heraldic devise by the kings of Anjou, Brittany, and was adopted by their descendant, Henry II of England. In Medieval times the shrub was known as 'Planta genista', giving rise to the royal family name of Plantagenet. Besides its heraldic fame, the broom also has a large number of medicinal uses not shared by the gorse. Though they are different plants with different properties, the cross-over in naming, and a general similarity, does mean that symbolically it can sometimes be difficult to disentangle the two.

Gorse/furze is the second of the five vowels of the Ogham alphabet and, along with the broom, is one of the eight Bramble Trees of the Brehon Law classification. It is mentioned in the '*Cad Goddeu*':

> *The furze was not well-behaved*
> *until he was tamed.....*

which may refer to the shrub's wild, uncultivated habitat or to the fact that it used to be 'tamed' by burning in order to produce young tender shoots for cattle to graze on. The burning would have been carried out in spring, around the Vernal Equinox.

Robert Graves' Tree Calendar attributes gorse to this festival because it begins to flower profusely in March, its bright flowers symbolizing the waxing sun after the darkness of winter. However, Liz and Colin Murray's *'The Celtic Tree Oracle'* associates it with the Celtic fire festival of Lughnasadh.

In the Welsh *'Mabinogion'* tale 'Math son of Mathonwy', Math and Gwydion create a bride from the flowers of oak, broom and meadowsweet, after Llew's mother Arianrhod has declared he shall not have a mortal wife. Through her link with the broom, the Flower-Bride, Blodeuwedd, is the Spring Maiden of the Equinox as well as being the May Queen of Beltane, symbol of the land's lush fruitfulness, while her marriage gives her a connection with Lughnasadh - dedicated to the Irish equivalent of Llew.

Pliny mentions that gorse was laid in water to catch gold dust carried by the current, using sympathetic magic in the hope that like would attract like. Gorse was also believed to be a remedy against jaundice, on the homeopathic principle that the yellow flowers resembled the yellowing complexion of someone with the disease.

A poem by Elizabeth Barrett Browning (1806-61) refers to a tale that when Linnëus first saw gorse growing in Britain he fell to his knees in awe:

> *Mountain gorses, since Linnëus*
> *Knelt beside you on the sod,*
> *For your beauty thanking God.......'"*

Earlier in the poem she sums up the essential teaching and symbolism of gorse:

*Mountain blossoms, shining blossoms,*
*Do ye teach us to be glad*
*When no summer can be had,*
*Blooming in our inward bosoms?*
*Ye, whom God preserveth still,*
*Set as lights upon a hill;*
*Tokens to the wintry earth that beauty liveth still."*

The plant's year round flowering also led to it being included in traditional bridal bouquets to represent everlasting love, and to the old folk saying:

*When Gorse is out of bloom,*
*Kissing's out of season.*

In the past, flaming gorse brands were carried amongst the cattle at Midsummer to purify them, bringing health and prosperity; and Gorse is generally thought of as propitious - the golden symbol of spring that offers spiritual strength throughout the year.


**Sources for quotes:**
1. Nash, D W - *'Taliesin, or the Bards and Druids of Britain'*
2. Holden, Edith - quoted in *'The Country Diary of an Edwardian Lady'*, Book Club Associates, London, 1977 ed.

Spring's herald challenges the spirit of winter,
who holds sway on the grey moor.
Though his power weakens hour by hour,
a chill host still lingers on stormy days,
in dark ragged cloaks
that hang from the shoulders of a lowering sky.


Ground is won and lost, and won again
as the strengthening force of summer
drives the old season back -
a host on white mares with flowing manes
riding high in the blue air.
And at Alban Eilir,
finally they celebrate victory,
descending on a colourless land
to kindle golden gorse flames
with sparks from their lord, the sun.

# Spring Equinox Celebration

On a table, or on the floor in the centre of a room, place a bright yellow cloth, yellow candles, flowering gorse and daffodils. Or, ideally, work outside in a secluded place, with lanterns in place of candles. Have a black and a white cloth in readiness, and a vessel of mead or other golden drink.

The Mabon, the Celtic Son of Light, who is worked with in this rite is a young god/hero associated with the waxing sun, hope and liberation.

If you wish, cast a sacred circle around your place of working and call upon the elemental energies of the four quarters to offer their guidance and guardianship.

Light the candles/lanterns, and still facing the altar say:

*Maiden of Spring,*
*who first stirred at Imbolc,*
*now, fully awake*
*and crowned with the flowers of the fields,*
*shyly you face*
*a proud noble youth:*
*the Mabon, named and armed.*
*In the soft sun that shines*
*like the golden gorse,*
*he tests his strength.*
*In each bud that opens*
*with cautious leaf*
*you smile.*
*Maid and Mabon,*
*hand in hand,*
*timid still,*
*you dance the gentle breeze.*
*Colour and song have returned to the land.*

Lay a black cloth in the west, a white cloth in the east. Step from the black onto the white and say:

> *As the sunwheel spins through the seasons,*
> *light and dark find perfect balance at this time,*
> *meeting at the threshold where light waxes*
> *and darkness wanes.*
> *I tread the year's path,*
> *drawing nearer*
> *to the greatest light at Alban Hefin* (the Summer Solstice).

This may be followed by a joyous sunwise circle dance. Afterwards face the altar again and say:

> *Balance is the way of the sacred*
> *in body, mind and soul,*
> *reflected in all creation:*
> *in earth and air*
> *water and fire,*
> *land and sky,*
> *flower and beast.*

Ask that the Maiden of Spring and the Mabon bless the vessel of mead, then raise it, saying:

> *I salute this season of light and warmth. May its power be felt in the hearts of all, bringing peace and hope into the world.*

Sit quietly for a while, visualizing a spring landscape where you speak with the Spring Maiden and youthful Mabon about your aspirations. Finally, give thanks, unwind the circle and pour the remainder of the mead on the earth as an offering.

A hillside carpeted with purple basks in the heat of the noonday sun.


Heather, Ur, Grug,
offering sweet nectar,
and Mid-summer's perfume.
Bringer of good fortune,
I come in peace and in search of wisdom.
My greetings and blessings to you and all your kin.
Is it your wish to share your knowledge and energy with me?

# Heather

Heather is an evergreen undershrub belonging to the *Ericaceae* family, and is closely related to the ling (*Calluna vulgaris*). It grows mainly on heaths and moors, preferring acidic soil, but will thrive in a range of habitats, including both damp and dry areas, bright sun or shade.

Bell Heather (*Erica cinerea*) reaches 40-50 cm, while Irish Heath (*Erica mediterranea*) can attain a much greater height. The small needle-like leaves of the common Bell Heather occur in groups of three and have curled edges to protect against water loss. In the wild, purple, and less frequently white, flowers appear during the summer, though some imported garden varieties are winter-flowering.

The heather is well-adapted for survival because if it fails to be pollinated by bees the stamens elongate, dispersing pollen on the wind. Survival is also ensured because the seeds can remain dormant in the ground for up to ten years until conditions are right for germination - the reason why large numbers of new plants spring up simultaneously after a heath fire to recolonize an area.

The Irish Brehon Law places heather in the category of Bramble, and as the second vowel of the Ogham alphabet it forms part of the 'sweet cauldron of five trees'. In Robert Graves' tree calendar it is assigned to the Summer Solstice or Alban Hefin, a time when the wild variety is in flower, the reddish-purple blossoms representing fertility, heat and passion.

Heather was sacred to the Roman and Sicilian love goddess, Venus Erycina, and dedications from the Roman period found in Switzerland refer to a Gallic heather-goddess - Uroica, whose name is etymologically related both to the Irish 'Ur' and to *'ereice'*, the Greek for heather. According to one tale, Venus Erycina's nymphs set up a hero-shrine on Mount Eryx for Butes the bee-master, showing a close connection between bees and heather in Sicilian myth; while amongst the early Celts there was a belief that the bee was a messenger travelling between the human realm and the Otherworld along the slanting rays of the sun.

'Heath' has given us the word 'Heathen', originally describing people in remote areas far from civilization who adhered to the old ways after the advent of Christianity. Folk-myth offers the reverse explanation that when Christian invaders slaughtered the Picts, their Heathen blood soaked the ground, transforming it into 'heath'.

The link between heather and the ancient Picts is found again in a story that takes place in the fourth century. It tells how Vikings killed all the native inhabitants of Shetland, sparing just a father and a son in the hope that they would reveal the formula for Pictish heather ale. But both men refused to speak, and only after prolonged torture did the father tell the enemy that he would now give them whatever information they wanted, providing his son was killed beforehand. This was done, though still the father would say nothing, except that he had feared his son would give way under torture and betray the secret, a secret he himself then took to the grave.

It is probably heather ale which is referred to in D W Nash's translation of the *'Cad Goddeu'*:

> *'The heath was giving consolation comforting the people.*

And though the original formula is lost, in the nineteenth century heather tops, blended with hops, ginger and syrup, were still used in a traditional Scottish beer, brewed in late summer.

Symbolically, white heather is untainted by the blood of battle, so it came to represent good fortune and protection against evil. Gypsies sell it for luck and Queen Victoria gave Princess Alexandra of Denmark, her future daughter-in-law, a lucky sprig, popularizing the custom. It was also believed that washing with water in which heather flowers had been infused, or in dew gathered from them at the full moon, preserved youthfulness and beauty.

Along with the power to evoke drowsy summer days and the freedom of wild open spaces, its lucky symbolism makes heather one of the most uplifting of the sacred trees.


**Sources for quotes:**
Nash, D W - *'Taliesin, or the Bards and Druids of Britain'*.

The clan are gathered
on the hill in celebration.
Beneath the Solstice sun
a multitude of rich cloaks gleam
in purple, green and white.


Chieftains extend hospitality
to the bright-robed bees,
offering a feast of nectar,
the precious honey mead.
Their feasting done, each guest then bears
tribal honour and words of prayer
to Lugh, the Shining One.


The noble company remains,
listening to the bard-wind's harp
and drinking toasts in perfumed rain,
'til purple and white cloaks are shed
and autumn declares the assembly's end.

# Summer Solstice Rite

Of all the seasonal festivals, the Summer Solstice (Alban Hefin) is best celebrated outside, under the rays of the sun at the moment of its greatest power - weather permitting. The following rite is designed to be performed around noon, the absolute peak of the solar year, after which the sun's strength slowly begins to decrease. A similar rite can be performed at dawn to greet the sun on the longest day.

The ideal place to work would be on open heathland, but do not light candles or a fire in case it gets out of control, besides, no flame kindled by human hand can compete with the Solstice sun itself. If you want to mark the quarters, place a suitable symbol at each cardinal point, for example a plain stone for north/earth, a feather for east/air, a red gemstone for south/fire and a shell for west/water.

If you are forced inside by rain, then a candle or group of candles can be used to represent the sun, and your sacred space can be decorated with heather and oak, also sacred to the Summer Solstice. Whether working in or out of doors, cut a bunch of heather and a leafy oak bough before starting the rite, remembering to show respect, and have some red ribbon in readiness.

Begin by giving honour to the Spirit of Place - of the heath - and, if you wish, cast a sacred circle and request the guardianship of the elemental powers.

Stand in silence for a moment inhaling the scent of the heather and feeling the heat of the sun on your skin, conscious that without it there would be no life. Then hold the oak bough high and say:

'Llew/Lugh, spirit behind the manifested sun, I salute you and ask your blessings on this rite of the Summer Solstice.

'At the darkest hour you were born from the womb of the night, to bring light and hope into the world. At Imbolc you stood alone, youthful yet bold; at Beltane you took Blodeuwedd for your Flower Bride; now, in your prime, you encourage *vibrant growth - leaves and blossoms and ripening corn.*

*'I celebrate your triumph over darkness.'*

Again appreciate the sun's gifts before continuing:

*'May I be filled with the strength, health and energy of Mid-summer. And may all realms: mineral, plant, animal and human, be blessed.'*

Raise the bunch of heather towards the sun, saying:

*'At the time of your greatest power I ask that your light enter into me so that it will shine within me throughout the year.'* Bind the heather with red ribbon while you continue to speak: *'As the heather wears its bright blossoms like the fire of the sun and of summer's passion, may it hold all that is positive in this moment.*

*'All nature is now at the height of colour and fertility, but it can grow no more, and your own strength has reached its peak. Change is imminent, the land stands at the threshold of the downward spiral into cold and dark, when you go to your rest in Annwn. Yet this heather will be a symbol of summer even at the darkest moments, and with it in my hand I will welcome your rebirth at the Winter Solstice and your return to strength through Imbolc and Beltane.'*

Again raise the oak bough, with the words:

*'Llew, Lord of Life. I give thanks for the abundance and the joy of summer.'*

Meditate on this for a while before thanking the elemental powers and unwinding the circle. Place the bunch of heather in a box in a cool dry place and keep it as a token of optimism until the sun is 'reborn' at the Winter Solstice.

Growing on exposed moorland, a delicate tree shimmers in a wind that heralds the approach of autumn.


Aspen, Edhadh, Aethnen,
leaves brightly dancing,
chanting in harmony.
Spirit messenger,
I come in peace and in search of wisdom.
My greetings and blessings to you and all your kin.
Is it your wish to share your knowledge and energy with me?

# Aspen

The aspen (*Populus tremula*) is a smallish member of the poplar family which rarely reaches more than 15m in height. It has silver-green bark and scallop-shaped leaves, darker above and pale green beneath, suspended from long stalks that cause them to flutter in the slightest breeze. In February or March, before the leaf-buds unfurl, male trees produce short silky catkins with purple anthers. The female catkins, which also appear during early spring, are green at first but become frothy white in May as they shed their seeds.

The aspen flourishes across a wide area, from the Arctic to the Mediterranean, favouring damp woodland, hedgerows and moors, and is able to thrive on a variety of soils.

Mythologically, aspen and white poplar (*Populus alba*) are largely interchangeable, though botanically they are separate varieties. Besides having a different outline - the white poplar is taller with a broader crown - the most obvious difference is that the poplar has deeply lobed leaves which are white underneath and lack the exceptionally long leaf-stalks of the aspen. A third variety, the grey poplar, probably a hybrid of the aspen and white poplar, has leaves with grey undersides, slightly less rounded in shape than those of the aspen.

Aspen/white poplar is the fourth vowel of the Ogham alphabet, and is classed as a Shrub according to the Irish Brehon Law. Robert Graves allocates it to the Autumn Equinox in his tree calendar, describing it as a tree of old age.

According to Greek myth, Hercules bound his brow with white poplar after killing the giant Cacus, who had stolen a herd of divine cattle - the fruit of the hero's tenth labour. It is said that the undersides of the leaves were bleached by the heat from his radiant forehead and have remained white ever since.

Poplar is also mentioned in the Greek myth of Phaeton, which tells how the son of the solar deity Apollo receives permission to drive the sun chariot in order to prove his divine parentage. Carried away by pride and excitement, he steers it too near the earth, causing rivers to dry up and vegetation to wither. Then, trying to avoid further destruction, the youth heads so far out into space that any plants which survived the heat now perish from extreme cold, and men cry out in despair. Their cries wake Zeus from a deep sleep, and when the chief god realizes that a mortal, daring to drive the sun chariot, is responsible for the disaster, he strikes Phaeton dead with a thunderbolt.

His three sisters, known as the Heliades, weep so bitterly for him that the gods, taking pity on them, transform them into 'white poplars', while their tears are turned into drops of amber, a substance sacred to Apollo.

The origins of this myth may lie in the fact that both amber and the aspen were brought from the north, though here a distinction must be made between aspen and white poplar, which have perhaps become confused or been amalgamated in the tale. The former is native to Britain, often occurring in ancient woodland, and was one of the first trees to re-colonize the islands following the last Ice Age. The latter is introduced and likely to have come from the area around Greece. Therefore aspen, not poplar, is probably also the tree which Hercules obtained from the Hyperboreans, or dwellers beyond the north wind, a people reputed to be devout worshippers of Apollo.

Mystery surrounds this mythical race, who are mentioned in Classical accounts such as that written by Hecataeus of Abdera between 300 and 200 BC, though it has been suggested that they were the Celtic inhabitants of Britain whose Druids officiated in the worship of a solar deity, identified by the Greeks with Apollo. It is possible that the aspen was particularly sacred to the Hyperboreans, as it was deemed worthy of taking to transplant in a far distant land.

Greek myth describes white poplar/aspen as growing in abundance around the River Styx, across which the dead must pass to Hades, and in the *Odyssey* it is mentioned as a tree of resurrection, along with the alder and cypress. This ties in with its solar symbolism, because though the sun is seen to 'die' each day, or to reach its nadir at the time of the Winter Solstice, it is always 'reborn'. And for the ancient Greeks, Apollo, lord of the sun, was at his most powerful at the time of the Summer Solstice when he dwelt in the northern realm of the Hyperboreans, the original home of the aspen.

As a timber once used to make shields, the tree is associated with outer protection. Medicinally, aspen/white poplar also protects - reducing fever and preventing thrombosis through the salicin in its bark.

Because of its responsiveness to the wind, aspen is linked with the element air, and the rustling of its leaves has given it the folk name of the 'whispering' or 'talking' tree, or 'Crann Critheac' in Irish Gaelic, translated as 'the quivering tree'. Air, in turn, is linked with life and spirit and the sacred word that brought about primal creation, while in many belief systems the wind is believed to carry divine messages. The aspen, with its ability to give voice to the invisible element, can therefore be seen as a revealer of Otherworldly wisdom.

## Inspiration

Listen to the whispering leaves.
At the misty twilight hour,
Wisdom's voice speaks through the trees.


Bright Knowledge trembling on the breeze,
Wears the poplar's silver crown.
Listen to the whispering leaves.


Like a storm that skims the seas,
And the Druid's dragon power,
Wisdom's voice speaks through the trees.


Softly the wanton wind weaves,
Its spell on bark and bough.
Listen to the whispering leaves.


A faery gift of aspen, wreaths
The Pen Beirdd's shining brow.
Wisdom's voice speaks through the trees.


Journeying in the forest frees,
The spirit of the Awen.
Listen to the whispering leaves,
Wisdom's voice speaks through the trees.

# The Whispering Tree

Go out in search of an aspen, in the physical rather than the inner realm, or you could work with a white or grey poplar instead; the latter 'whispers' in a similar way to the aspen so makes a good alternative. You need to ensure that the tree grows in a relatively secluded place, and bring a snack with you to earth yourself after meditating.

You will hear the unmistakable musical rustle and swish of the leaves some distance away, calling you. Approach the tree with reverence, offer a suitable greeting and pause for a moment to sense if it is open to human contact. If you feel welcome, sit or stand with your back against the trunk and close your eyes, allowing the sound of the leaves to act like a mantra, altering consciousness.

Without trying too hard, which will prevent the inner senses from opening, listen to what the leaves are telling you: the answer to a question or problem; changes that could be made in your life; a song or poem..........

Continue for as long as it feels right, then gradually return to ordinary consciousness, take several deep breaths and open your eyes. Give yourself time to re-adjust to your surroundings before giving thanks to the tree and perhaps making a personal offering. Finally, eat something to earth yourself fully.

By the wall of an old churchyard, a dark tree casts its shadow across the headstones.


Yew, Ido, Ywen,
your robe emerald green,
your jewels, scarlet berries.
Most ancient of trees,
I come in peace and in search of wisdom.
My greetings and blessings to you and all your kin.
Is it your wish to share your knowledge and energy with me?

# Yew

The yew (*Taxus baccata*) forms a squat outline, with a broad trunk and widely spreading crown of evergreen foliage. The dark needle-like leaves are flattened and have a marked central groove, and the bark is reddish and flaky in texture. Between February and April the flowers appear, the male and female on separate trees, followed by mat red fruits or arils, each containing a single seed at the base of an open cup. They are deadly poisonous, though the poison is in the seed, not the flesh; the leaves, too, are poisonous and dangerous to grazing cattle.

In the wild, the yew flourishes on the chalk downs of southern England and on limestone hills in the north and west. It is native to the British Isles, and has grown here since the end of the last Ice Age; it also occurs widely on the Continent, from Norway to Central Europe.

The most long-lived of trees, in theory a yew could survive for ever because of an ability to rejuvenate itself in a number of different ways: through the generation of cambium (a layer under the surface bark which forms new cells) to cover 'dead wood'; by creating a new trunk from a linked circle of younger trunks growing from the foot of the original one; by producing roots at the base of branches, which extend through the decaying trunk into the earth, and by sending out roots from low-hanging branches when they touch the ground. As these remain attached to the parent tree, a whole grove can be formed by one yew, the offspring living on after the old tree 'dies'.

Experts have dated the yew at Linton in Herefordshire, with its 33ft girth, to at least 4000 years old, while another, at Discoed in Powys, is said to have reached the age of 5000 years.

The Irish Brehon Law classifies the yew as one of the seven trees of Chieftain status because of:

'*its noble structures;* (That is, the highly prized pieces of furniture manufactured from it.)'

And though not listed here, bows were commonly made from yew wood, giving the tree the Latin name *'Taxus baccata'* from *'toxon'* - the Greek for bow, and *'toxicon'* - the Greek for the poison with which arrows were tipped. In ancient Ireland yew also formed part of the mixture used to poison weapons.

Its poisonous nature, combined with strength, longevity and great powers of renewal made yew the primary tree of death and rebirth for the ancient Celts, and apart from the oak, the species most sacred to the Druids. The five magical trees of ancient Ireland, mentioned in the *'Metrical Dindsenchas'* (place name tales), include the Bole of Ross, a yew described as stately and flawless.

It was known as 'the renown of Banbha', linking it to a goddess who, together with Fodla and Eriu, symbolized the land. In *'The White Goddess'* we find the concept of a triple goddess with the aspects of maid, mother and crone, associated respectively with the three visible phases of the moon. According to this belief, widespread in twentieth century paganism, Banbha represents the crone or death aspect of the threefold deity of Ireland.

Robert Graves' tree calendar allocates yew to Samhain, the end of the Pagan Celtic year, a time when the veil between our world and the Other is thin, allowing spirits to pass easily across the threshold. Yew is also the tree of the Nameless Day, the shortest, darkest day of the year before the sun is reborn at the Winter Solstice (Alban Arthan in Welsh).

Yews are still found in most graveyards, supposedly to stop ghosts from wandering and to protect the dead from graverobbers or witches, but churchyard yews often pre-date the Christian church and may mark an earlier Pagan sacred site. Allen Meredith, an expert who has spent many years studying yews, discovered that when the Saxons built their church at Tandridge, Surrey, they included a nearby yew beneath the stone vaulting, proof of the tree's greater age and the reverence in which it was held. Therefore, the Christians inherited the ancient symbol of death and rebirth, in turn seeing it as a tree of resurrection associated with the Day of Judgement when the dead would rise again.

The Irish tragedy *'The Fate of the Sons of Usna'*, found in *'Celtic Myths and Legends'* by C W Rolleston, ends with the death of Deirdre and her lover Naisi. The story tells that a yew tree grew from each of their graves and in time met over the church of Armagh, the boughs intertwining so no one could separate them.

*'The White Goddess'* contains a slightly different version - that the two trees sprouted from yew stakes driven through the lovers' hearts to keep their ghosts apart.

Though generally regarded as a graveyard tree, yews can sometimes be found at sites of historical and archaeological interest like the Chalice Well Gardens, Glastonbury, where excavations in the vicinity of the well unearthed the root of a yew estimated to have been alive around AD 300. As it stands in line with living yew trees, it may once have formed part of a processional way that led to the well/spring, in Celtic tradition linked not only with healing but with initiation: symbolic death and rebirth.

The yew was also revered by the Anglo-Saxons and Norse, and was sacred to Woden/Odin - god of the dead, magical power and wisdom. Some sources describe the Norse World Tree, on which he hung to gain knowledge of the runes, as a yew, though it is more often said to be an ash.

Traditionally, yew is the most suitable wood for carving runes, and it has given its name to Eoh - Anglo-Saxon Futhorc/Eihwaz - Elder Futhark, known as the death rune. However, none of the rune poems contain this interpretation. The 'Old English Rune Poem' (early 9th century) describes yew as a 'joy on the estate'", the 'Old Norwegian rune Rhyme' (12th century) as 'the greenest wood in winter'" and the 'Old Icelandic Rune Poem' (dating from around the 15th century, but preserving older oral lore) as 'a strung bow'".

From ancient times to the present day, the yew is both guardian and teacher. The dark symbol of death, but bearing the red berry, the drop of life blood, it reminds us that the patterns of existence are cyclical, that each ending holds the seed of a new beginning.

## Sources for Quotes
1. Commissioners for Publishing the Ancient Laws and Institutes of Ireland - *'Ancient Laws of Ireland, Vol IV'*.
2. Thorsson, Edred - *'Runelore'*.

By grassy mound
and sacred spring,
by graveyard stone,
lichen stained,
yews drape their guardian shade -
a dark leafy pall
for the house of the dead,
where Banbha offers hospitality
in a poison draft drunk
from a red chalice berry.
Probing roots embrace her guest
to a raven serenade,
through the gates of Samhain.


Vaulted, seasonless green,
as winter strips and fades
each living thing.
Most ancient of trees,
watcher of ages,
who sees the acorn fall
and sprout and fruit; sees
the giant that held the skies
shrunken to a rotting bole,
crumbled to earth,
the dark lady's couch.
Under grassy mound
and graveyard stone,
the feast of root and worm,
the guest smiles, and
leaving flesh and bone as a parting gift,
throws the gates wide -
refreshed, bright as the sacred spring,
seeing with new eyes.

# Yew Journey

The following journey, based on personal experience, is given as an example to show one of the many ways to work with the yew:

Soon after entering the inner forest, I made contact with the guide I normally work with, her face serene in the leafy half-light. She indicated for me to follow her along a path almost hidden by bracken, past oak and beech to an ancient yew that filled the air with its sharp resinous scent.

Tracing the Ogham sign of Ido in the air towards it, I offered greetings and, when I experienced a sense of acceptance, laid my hands on the trunk to create a link, saying:

'I request inspiration in word, music or image, if it is your will.'

Before I had time to pick up a response, my guide stepped between myself and the tree, no longer alone but with a wolf to her right, a black sow to her left and a raven perched on each shoulder of her deep green cloak. Taking both my hands, she said:

'As guardian of this grove, I carry the spirit of the yew. Go forward in peace.'

I looked past her at the narrow gap in the trunk that I would have to step through, then met her eyes again and asked if I could take a companion, choosing the wolf. It is a ferocious animal, yet accompanied me calmly, with no hint of menace, giving rise to the thought, 'This is how death walks at our side.'

Beyond the gateway I discovered a flight of stairs that spiralled downward, vanishing into darkness far below. Sometimes the wolf led the way, sometimes I walked ahead, but still we descended, deeper and deeper into the earth, until we reached a series of underground halls where it was just light enough to see that the roof was supported by mighty yew roots.

Totally preoccupied by my surroundings, at first I failed to notice the blackened, decomposing corpse which had appeared out of the gloom, and was now approaching with an outstretched hand. Strangely, I was not repulsed by it, simply curious. So I clasped the hand that was offered, to find a young red-haired woman standing where the corpse had been a second earlier, her full lips smiling in welcome. Her hand was still holding mine, her smile still bright, when an arrow struck me, but there was no pain and it passed harmlessly through my heart, bringing a sense of renewal.

Uplifted, I walked down arched passages with the wolf padding at my side, continuing to the farthest recess of the underground palace, where a figure was seated on a throne of gnarled wood overhung with branches. Her robes were green, her veil black, and through it I saw the shadowy impression of haggard features.

I bowed before her, my mind reeling with thoughts of death and rebirth. For a long while I remained there, motionless, struggling to stop the chatter of my inner voice, then finally looked up.

'Death, sleep, winter,' the woman whispered.

After a pause I ventured to speak. 'I wish to learn. What do you require of me?'

Her response was a barely perceptible movement of her hand, drawing my attention to the red jewel she held, making me aware that my journey had become a quest, a search for riches in uncharted realms. She said nothing, though her gesture left me in no doubt that she intended me to take the gift.

The moment I did so, everything was plunged into utter blackness except for a red glow cast by the jewel, shining like a faint ray of hope amidst chaos.

I turned, with the wolf at my side, conscious that I carried something invaluable as I traced my way back along the passages and up the stairway. It had seemed long before, but now spiralled endlessly, so my head - or my whole self - was spinning. Again, I had to still my thoughts in order to find the presence of mind to continue.

Resigning myself, I climbed on and at last found my way out into the forest, the jewel-light in my hand now transformed into a red cup-shaped berry.

With deepest thanks, I placed it on the earth at the foot of the yew, visualizing the potential tree.........new life.

Burnished by the setting sun, an ancient tree presides over a woodland of copper and gold.

Beech, Phagos, Ffawydden,
noble upholder of tradition.
Autumn's antique leaves
lingering to guard the soft shoots of spring.
I come in peace and in search of wisdom.
My greetings and blessings to you and all your kin.
Is it your wish to share your knowledge and energy with me?

# Beech

The beech *(Fagus sylvatica)* is native to southern England and Wales where it has grown since the end of the last Ice Age. It is often found in ancient woodland, usually on chalk or limestone, though it also occurs in sandy areas. As its root system aerates the soil and the leaves contain a large amount of potash, beech improves fertility and helps support surrounding trees, though the leaf litter lies thick on the ground for long periods, discouraging undergrowth.

The beech has smooth grey bark and oval leaves with a pointed tip, which are bright green in summer and turn a vivid copper in autumn. They remain on young trees throughout the winter into spring, side by side with the long narrow leaf buds. In April yellow flowers appear - the male flowers forming on catkins, the female in clusters on short stalks. These develop into triangular nuts protected by a thick hairy covering, known as mast.

Beech is often cultivated as an ornamental tree, especially the maroon-leaved Copper Beech, and because of its rapid growth is popular for hedging. It is also a good timber for making light furniture and small items such as bowls.

In the past, the smooth close-grained wood of the beech was used for runic inscriptions, which despite their perishable nature occasionally survive, while documentary evidence is found in the writings of the sixth century bishop and poet Venantius Fortunatus who said, 'Let the barbarian rune be marked on beechwood tablets'. This ancient connection with writing has led to an etymological link between the tree's name and the word for 'book' in Teutonic languages like English. For the same reason, beech came to be associated with learning and the preservation of traditional lore.

The Latin name for the beech *'Fagus'* derives from the Greek 'to eat', referring to the edible mast which provided the staple food of wild boar and of the domesticated swine that were once allowed to roam the common woodland, and which

still feeds parkland deer. 'Faggot', meaning fire-wood, in turn derives from 'fagus', as beech makes an excellent fuel.

The Ogham letter Phagos was the first of five extra letters added after the original twenty, so beech is not given a moon-th or sacred day in Graves' tree calendar. Nor does it occur in the Irish Brehon Law tree classification.

The *'Cad Goddeu'* says:

*Putting forth new leaves are the tops of the beech,
Changing form and being renewed from a withered state;.....*

and:   *Prosperous the beech tree.......,"*

evoking a sense of fertility, plenty, and rebirth, just as traditional lore kept alive by each generation is constantly renewed.

In Rome beeches were sacred to the goddess Diana, and in the first century AD a beech that grew in her grove in the Alban Hills was honoured by kissing and embracing its trunk, lying beneath its shade and making a libation of wine. The Franks also revered the beech tree, and consulted a beech oracle. It is possible that the Achaeans who settled Greece followed a similar practice, but when they found no beeches in their new homeland they turned to the oak instead. This may explain why the oak at Dodona is referred to as *'phagus'*, equivalent to *'fagus'*, rather than as *'drus'* (oak). The beech, like the oak, was seen as regal and bore the title Queen of the Woods, partner to the oak - King of the Woods.

Perhaps due to its link with the feminine, and so with fertility, or perhaps because it is one of the best fire-woods, a beech tree provided the focus for a Prussian folk custom that took place on the first Sunday of Lent. A bar of wood was fixed to the tree to form a cross, and after straw and brushwood had been piled at its foot, it was set alight, sometimes containing a straw effigy. The celebrants then circled the burning tree, carrying lighted torches and praying. Like many local traditions, with their Christian gloss, this custom was clearly the remnant of a Pagan fertility rite performed at sowing time to purify the fields with fire, banish evil spirits and propitiate the gods.

From sacred tree and guardian of ancestral lore, to provider of food for animals and warmth in the domestic hearth, the beech sustains on all levels - spiritual, mental and physical.

**Sources for Quotes:**
1. Graves, Robert - *'The White Goddess'*.
2. Nash, D W (trans.) - *'Taliesin, or the Bards and Druids of Britain'*.

Roots reach through the ages
into ancestral land.
Leaves are written with the words
of a wise and ancient hand.
Every branch of knowledge
spreading from one trunk,
where the sap of understanding
is drawn up from the past.
Unfurling schemes and dreams,
crowned with green and gold,
boughs that bear tomorrow's fruit,
the ripening seeds of hope -
all reach upward for the sky,
tight-curled bud, eager shoot,
yet the source of each lies in the earth
in one silent sacred root.

# Walking the Beech Wood Path

The purpose of 'the beech wood path' is to explore an aspect of your heritage, becoming aware of its importance to the present, and the chain of continuity. Possible lines for exploration are: family history, the history and legends of the town/area where you live, the historical and mythological traditions of your occupation, for example medicine or one of the arts.

The path can be taken either as an inner journey or walked in a physical beech wood whilst in a state of meditation. Whichever you chose, enter the wood with reverence, focusing on your inner purpose as well as on your surroundings: the scent of earth and leaf mould, the colour of the leaves, the crunch of mast beneath your feet, a glimpse of bird or beast........... Feel the presence of the trees, who have watched the centuries pass and whose ancestors have given their wood for humankind to record names and events and to inscribe sacred runes.

Before you begin, ask the blessings of the spirit of the wood, and ensure that you are welcome and feel secure. Do the same for each of the trees that you work with.

When you find one that feels appropriate, approach and offer your greetings. Then stand with your back to it, feeling its support, or sit at its foot. This first tree represents the present. Meditate on your subject in its current state, both positive and negative, and the part you yourself play in it..............Take your time, and when you have finished remember to give thanks.

At the second tree meditate on the recent past. What has changed? How have the characters/events of this period influenced the present? How have they affected you?

And so, stage by stage, you step back along the path of history and tradition, even into the realms of myth, far before historical record. Whenever you do not wish to explore any further, simply stop and meditate on all the stages as a continuous story, starting from the time you have reached and moving forward to the present. Then, offer thanks and resume everyday consciousness. If you are also walking the path in the material world now focus only on your physical surroundings, especially on the solid earth beneath your feet, to ensure that you are fully grounded.

Before leaving the wood, inner or outer, return to the first tree you worked with, and after giving honour and sensing it is willing, cut a small piece from a branch. Trim it down to a suitable length and remove the bark, creating a smooth surface on which to carve one word that sums up what you learnt through meditation. Preferably use Ogham signs, runes or another sacred alphabet.

On the topmost branch of a gnarled apple tree, a cluster of golden-green foliage is studded with translucent berries:


Mistletoe, An t-uil-çoc, Uchelwydd,
plant most sacred,
bearing life's pearly seed.
All-heal of the Druids,
I come in peace and in search of wisdom.
My greetings and blessings to you and all your kin.
Is it your wish to share your knowledge and energy with me?

# Mistletoe

Mistletoe (*viscum album*) is an evergreen parasitic plant most frequently found on apple trees, though it can grow on hawthorn, ash, poplar and willow, and occasionally on oak. It has small flowers, arranged in groups of three, with male and female on separate plants, and white translucent berries containing a single seed surrounded by sticky juice. These provide one of the main food sources for the mistle thrush and are propagated by it wiping its seed-encrusted beak onto the branch of a new host tree.

The Druids regarded mistletoe as supremely sacred, especially if growing on an oak, though a reverence for mistletoe in combination with oak seems to go back as far as the Bronze Age according to evidence from a burial at Gristhorpe, Yorkshire which produced the remains of both. This reinforces a theory that the Druids inherited many of their practices from the pre-Celtic inhabitants of Britain - said by classical writers to be the original home of druidry, where apprentice Druids from Gaul were sent for instruction.

There is also evidence for the ritual use of mistletoe during the late Iron Age, based on the discovery of a man at Lindow Moss, Cheshire, whose stomach contained traces of its berries. Known as Lindow Man, he is thought to have died as a human sacrifice, and it has been suggested that he was a member of the nobility who willingly went to his death in the hope of saving his land from the Roman invaders in the 1st century AD.

The importance of both oak and mistletoe to the Gaulish Druids is mentioned by the Roman writer Pliny (AD 23-79) in his '*Natural History*':

'The druids.........held nothing more sacred than the mistletoe and the tree that bears it, always supposing that tree to be the oak.........In fact, they think that everything that grows on it has been sent from heaven and is a proof that the tree was chosen by the god himself.'

Pliny's account continues with a detailed description of the ritual gathering of mistletoe:

*'The mistletoe, however, is found but rarely upon the oak; and when found, is gathered with due religious ceremony, if possible on the sixth day of the moon (for it is by the moon that they* (the Druids) *measure their months and years, and also their ages of thirty years). They choose this day because the moon, though not yet in the middle of her course, has already considerable influence.......... Having made preparation for sacrifice and a banquet beneath the trees, they bring thither two white bulls, whose horns are bound then for the first time. Clad in a white robe, the priest ascends the tree and cuts the mistletoe with a golden sickle, and it is received by others in a white cloak. Then they kill the victims, praying that God will render this gift of his propitious to those to whom he has granted it.'*

Because of its parasitic nature, mistletoe grows without contacting the earth, making it a plant of sky and thunder deities. In the Druid rite described by Pliny, great care is taken to ensure that the bough does not touch the ground, or its power would be dissipated.

The mistletoe, bearing fruit which is at its ripest in the depths of winter, was a symbol of fertility, and the berries with their white sticky juice may have represented male sperm, though they probably had both solar and lunar connections. As they form the berries are greenish, they then become white and pearly like the full moon, but at the peak of ripeness take on a golden colour, reminiscent of the pale winter sun. The sickle used to cut the mistletoe was of gold, a masculine solar metal, curved in the shape of the female crescent moon. It is possible, therefore, that the ceremony was intended to unite the powers of male and female deities at a time of year when the land lay apparently dead and the sun was at its weakest, inviting an increase of strength to both earth and sky: the rebirth of vegetation and of the sun at the Solstice, represented in Celtic myth by the Mabon - the child of light.

Before the advent of Christianity evergreens were used to decorate homes and temples for the Midwinter rites, a custom at first banned by the young church because of its Pagan associations. But the ancient traditions of the people continued until greenery was officially permitted inside Christian homes. Holly, ivy, bay and other greenery also decked churches over Christmas, yet mistletoe was forbidden, and even today it is never hung inside a church. Exceptions to the rule occurred at York Minster where, during Medieval times, a mistletoe bough was laid on the high altar over the twelve days of Christmas, heralding a period of peace and universal pardon in the city; and at the Collegiate Church in Wolverhampton, where it was blessed before being distributed to the people.

It is still thought unlucky to cut mistletoe except at Christmas, and the Celtic association with fertility has survived through the ages in the custom of kissing beneath it. The Christmas Tree, which had become popular in England by the late nineteenth century, took the place of the Kissing Bough, an evergreen garland containing mistletoe that was hung from the ceiling and decorated with red apples, coloured paper and candles. In areas where actual mistletoe was unavailable, the entire garland was referred to as 'the mistletoe' and associated with the same traditional customs.

According to Pliny, the Druids called the plant 'all-heal', and it was believed to be an antidote to poison, to make barren cattle fertile, and to act as a general bringer of good health. One of several conditions which he claims can be helped by taking it is epilepsy, in the past attributed to spirit possession, indicating that the sacred 'all-heal' was also thought to have power over intruding spirits.

Any internal medicine cannot have included the berries which are deadly poisonous, though the leaves and twigs have the property of relaxing the nervous system and may be effective against cancer. Pliny noted that mistletoe could reduce tumours, and modern medical research has gone some way towards confirming this.

In Celtic myth, cauldrons are linked with the theme of re-birth, either after death, or the symbolic rebirth of initiation, as mistletoe itself is linked with the sun's death and rebirth from the Underworld in the druidic Winter Solstice rite. The poem 'Preiddeu Annwn' ('The Spoils of Annwn'), ascribed to the Bard Taliesin, tells how King Arthur and his companions undertake a quest to win:

> '.......the cauldron of the Chief of Annwn..........
> With a ridge round its edge of pearls......"

Considering the plant's mythological associations, and the fact that it formed part of the sacred meal eaten by Lindow Man shortly before his sacrifice and journey into the Underworld (Annwn), it is possible that the 'pearls' described are in fact mistletoe berries.

Mistletoe does not appear in the Irish Brehon Law tree classification, nor is it given an Ogham letter, presumably because it was not of this world but set apart, supremely sacred and secret - a symbol of the inner mysteries; and, in later times, unmentionable because of its esoteric Pagan links.

The Norse peoples also recognized mistletoe as unique, and it is central to the myth of the solar god Balder:

After he experienced premonitory dreams, Balder's mother Frigga made all things, including every mineral, plant and animal, swear they would not harm him, though she ignored the mistletoe growing on an oak at the gates of Valhalla as it seemed too small to pose any threat.

Because of his apparent invulnerability to wounding, the gods entertained themselves by casting weapons at Balder. He remained unhurt until Loki the trickster gave a spear made of mistletoe wood to the blind god Hodur, who in innocence threw it, bringing about Balder's death - which symbolically occurred at the Summer Solstice.

The Druids probably cut the mistletoe around the Winter

Solstice, when the berries are ripe, Pliny does not say, though in *'The Golden Bough'* J G Frazer claims that they cut it at Midsummer, at the height of the sun's power. In historical times mistletoe was certainly gathered at Midsummer in Scandinavia, to coincide with the lighting of fires known as Balder's balefires.

Frazer goes on to put forward his theory that Balder was an oak god, the personification of the oak, and that the mistletoe embodied his spirit. He states that the ancients, seeing the evergreen mistletoe on the deciduous oak, may have believed it to be the source of the oak's life. Therefore, cutting the mistletoe deprives Balder of his source of life. In early belief the object/plant containing a person's life, in effect also contained their death, as this was the inevitable result of the destruction of the object. Frazer writes: 'Hence if a man's death is in an object, it is perfectly natural that he should be killed by a blow from it.'

The title of *'The Golden Bough'* derives from a poetic name for a plant believed to be the mistletoe which, according to Virgil, the Sibyl instructed Aeneas to break before journeying to the Underworld. In classical times, a unique custom took place at the goddess Diana's sanctuary at Nemi, where a runaway slave was permitted to try and pluck a certain branch, identified with the Golden Bough, in order to win the right to single combat with her priest. If he was victorious he supplanted the existing priest, known as the King of the Wood, until he too was overthrown. Symbolically, the priest could only be killed once his life force, held within the mistletoe, had been taken.

Commenting on Frazer's work, Robert Graves gives the alternative suggestion that the breaking of the mistletoe bough implied the castration of Diana's priest by his successor - as in classical myth, where the god Cronos castrates his father Uranus - depriving the King of the Wood of his life-giving fertility rather than of his life-spirit.

The rite at Nemi is used by Frazer as an example to prove the central thesis of his book: the universality of the ancient priest-king, whose person represented the health of the land and people and embodied the power of their chief deity, and who would be ritually sacrificed before his strength and potency began to wane. In this context, the druidic Winter Solstice rite may have symbolized the death of the old sun-god, who then descended into the Underworld, and his replacement by (or rebirth as) a new sun-god: young and virile.

Lindow Man's death, like that of Balder or the priest at Nemi, was presaged by cutting the mistletoe, which he consumed in a sacred meal. Did he revive an archaic custom, dying as a sacrificial priest/king because his land was in crisis, indicating that his own strength had failed?

To the Celts, Norse, Greeks and Romans, mistletoe was representative of life: of the immortal spirit and the power of fertility. And though, over the centuries, its symbolism and rites have become diluted, it has never quite lost its ancient associations.

**Sources for Quotes:**

1. Kendrick, T D - *'The Druids: a Study in Celtic Prehistory'*
2. Nash, D W - *'Taliesin, or the Bards and Druids of Britain'*
3. Frazer, J G - *'The Golden Bough'*

# The Druid Apprentice and the Mistletoe

All day have I journeyed,
from dawn to rise of moon,
searching, searching for some sign,
to know my way is true.


An ancient branch my throne,
I, its royal crown.
I am lord above all plants,
my roots touch not the ground.


Beneath a tree I rest awhile,
limbs weary to the bone,
when wonder of wonders, I see above
mistletoe growing upon an oak.


Traveller, hold to your path,
though it may be sheer and long,
for I am the spirit of sky and sun,
and the tears of the wandering moon.


Much have I quested, and questioned
the wisdom of bird, beast and stone,
but of all you are wisest.  Speak again,
your voice speaks with the voice of my soul.

My message is peace, though once I slew.
I am life in the darkest hour.
As the sun steps anew through Midwinter's gate
I garland the Mabon's brow.

The gate through which I too must step,
when the blackness of wintry fear
will fall like your bough to the golden blade,
and the tracks of the youth pave a Druid's way.

# Winter Solstice Celebration

Set up an altar with seasonal decorations of evergreen, including mistletoe, as usual cutting any branches with sensitivity and gratitude. Light two candles for illumination and place a third, unlit, candle in the centre of the altar to represent the Mabon. Alternatively, it is very evocative to work outside using lanterns and with a small fire laid in readiness to be kindled.

To emphasize the sacred time and place you may like to cast a circle around your working area. You may also wish to invite the elemental energies of the four quarters to offer their guardianship.

When you have done this, face the altar and say:

'All is dark,
the earth frozen hard,
ice on every pool.
The wind blows bitter through bare branches,
like the sighs of the Great Mother who mourns her Lord,
whose death has left the world cold, without light,
as her belly swells with his child.

'In darkness the earth waits.
The Mother waits.
I/We wait.........'

Extinguish the candles/lanterns and say:

'The longest night of the year has fallen,
like the darkness of Annwn
where the Lord reposes
beyond the portals of the yew.'

Take a few minutes to meditate on the darkness, and on the rebirth of the sun. When you feel ready say:

'But each year, from the darkness light is born.
(Light the Mabon candle/kindle the fire).
Joy takes the place of sorrow,
hope replaces despair.
Brightness comes with the child of light - the Mabon.'

Light the other candles from the Mabon candle/re-light the lanterns with a twig from the fire, then pick up a piece of mistletoe and say:

'Seed of life
from a world between worlds.
Once cut with a sickle:
gold of the sun
crescent of the moon,
in union.
As above, so below,
I celebrate the cycle renewed.

'May the waxing sun bring happiness, strength and health to all, and peace and harmony throughout the world.'

If you wish, sit in meditation on the new light and new hopes for the coming year. Finally, give thanks to the gods, the elemental powers and spirits of the evergreens before concluding the rite by unwinding the circle.

# Bibliography

Bromwich, R. - *'Welsh Triads'*, University of Wales Press, Cardiff, 1978.
Commissioners for Publishing the Ancient Laws and Institutes of Ireland - *'Ancient Laws of Ireland, Vol IV'*, A. Thom & Co, Dublin; Longmans & Co, London, 1879.
Common Ground - *'Apple Games and Customs'*, Common Ground, London, 1994.
Fitter, A - *'Trees'*, HarperCollins, Glasgow, 1980.
Frazer, J G - *'The Golden Bough'*, Papermac, Macmillan, London, 1987 edition.
Geoffrey of Monmouth - *'The History of the Kings of Britain'*, Lewis Thorpe (trans.), Penguin Classics, London, 1966.
Graves, Robert - *'The White Goddess'*, Faber & Faber, London, 1961.
Green, Miranda J. - *'Exploring the World of the Druids'*, Thames and Hudson, London, 1997.
Grieve, M - *'A Modern Herbal'*, Tiger Books, London, 1998 edition.
Guerber, H A - *'Greece and Rome: Myths and Legends'*, Senate, London, 1994 edition.
Guerber, H A - 'The Norsemen', Senate, London, 1994 edition.
Guest, Charlotte - *'Mabinogion Legends'*, Llanerch, Lampeter, 1992.
Guest, Charlotte - *'Mabinogion - The Four Branches'*, Llanerch, Lampeter, 1990.
Holden, Edith - *'The Country Diary of an Edwardian Lady'*, Book Club Associates, London, 1977 edition.
Hole, Christina - *'British Folk Customs'* - Hutchinson Publishing, London, 1976.
Jackson, Kenneth (ed.) - *'Studies in Early Celtic Nature Poetry'*, Llanerch, Lampeter, 1995.
James, D and Bostock, S - *'Celtic Connections'*, Blandford, London, 1996.
Jordan, Michael - *'Plants of Mystery and Magic'*, Blandford, London, 1997.
Joyce, P W (trans.) - *'Old Celtic Romances'*, Longmans, Green & Co, London, 1920.
Kendrick, T D - *'Druids, or a Study in Celtic Prehistory'* - reprint by Kessinger Publishing, www.kessinger.net
Kipling, Rudyard - *'Puck of Pook's Hill'*, Macmillan, London, 1927.
MacDonald, Iain (ed.) - *'Saint Brendan'*, Floris Books, Edinburgh, 1992.
Malory, Sir Thomas - Le Morte D'Arthur, Wordsworth Editions Ltd, Ware, Herts, 1996.
Matthews, John - *'Taliesin: Shamanism and the Bardic Mysteries in Britain and Ireland'*, Aquarian, London, 1991.

Meehan, Aidan - *'Celtic Design - Spiral Patterns'*, Thames and Hudson, 1996.
Morganwg, I (compiled by), Probert, W (trans) Smith, Malcolm (intro) - *'The Triads of Britain'*, Wildwood House, London, 1977.
Murray, Liz & Colin - *'The Celtic Tree Oracle'*, Rider, London, 1988.
Nash, D W - *'Taliesin, or the Bards and Druids of Britain'* - reprint by Kessinger Publishing, www.kessinger.net
Pennar, Meirion (trans.) - *'The Black Book of Carmarthen'*, Llanerch, Lampeter, 1989.
Press, B - *'Trees of Britain and Europe'*, New Holland Publishers, London, 1992.
Rolleston, T W - *'Celtic Myths and Legends,'* Bracken Books, London.
Shakespeare, William - *'The Complete Works of Shakespeare'*, Odhams Press Ltd and Basil Blackwell, 1947.
Stewart, R J - *'Celtic Gods, Celtic Goddesses'*, Blandford, London, 1990.
Stewart, R J - *'Merlin: The Prophetic Vision and The Mystic Life'*, Arkana, London, 1994.
Tennyson, Alfred Lord - *'The Works of Alfred Tennyson'*, Kegan Paul, Trench, & Co, London, 1883.
Thorsson, Edred - *'Runelore'*, Samuel Weiser Inc., Maine, USA, 1987.
Valiente, Doreen - *'An ABC of Witchcraft, Past and Present'*, Robert Hale, London, 1986.
Wallis Budge, E A - *'Egyptian Magic'*, Arkana, London, 1988.

# Contacts and Organizations

Common Ground, 41 Shelton Street, London, WCEH 9HJ - Runs Save Our Orchards Campaign, promotes Apple Day, publishes books on trees, and encourages an interest in all aspects of 'local distinctiveness', eg. social history, folklore, customs, etc.

The Conservation Foundation, 1 Kensington Gore, London, SW7 2AR. Tel: 0207 591 3111.

The Woodland Trust, Autumn Park, Grantham, Lincolnshire, NG31 6LL. Tel: 01476 581111. Works to preserve ancient woodland and to create new woods. Membership includes newsletter, list of Woodland Trust Woods and information on native trees.

# FREE DETAILED CATALOGUE

Capall Bann is owned and run by people actively involved in many of the areas in which we publish. A detailed illustrated catalogue is available on request, SAE or International Postal Coupon appreciated. **Titles can be ordered direct from Capall Bann,** by post (cheque or PO with order), via our web site **www.capallbann.co.uk** using credit/debit card or Paypal, or from good bookshops and specialist outlets.

A Soul is Born by Eleyna Williamson
Angels and Goddesses - Celtic Christianity & Paganism, M. Howard
The Art of Conversation With the Genius Loci, Barry Patterson
Arthur - The Legend Unveiled, C Johnson & E Lung
Auguries and Omens - The Magical Lore of Birds, Yvonne Aburrow
Asyniur - Women's Mysteries in the Northern Tradition, S McGrath
Beginnings - Geomancy, Builder's Rites & Electional Astrology, Nigel Pennick
Between Earth and Sky, Julia Day
The Book of Seidr, Runic John
Caer Sidhe - Celtic Astrology and Astronomy, Michael Bayley
Call of the Horned Piper, Nigel Jackson
Can't Sleep, Won't Sleep, Linda Louisa Dell
Carnival of the Animals, Gregor Lamb
Cat's Company, Ann Walker
Celebrating Nature, Gordon MacLellan
Celtic Faery Shamanism, Catrin James
Celtic Lore & Druidic Ritual, Rhiannon Ryall
Celtic Sacrifice - Pre Christian Ritual & Religion, Marion Pearce
Celtic Saints and the Glastonbury Zodiac, Mary Caine
Circle and the Square, Jack Gale
Come Back To Life, Jenny Smedley
Company of Heaven, Jan McDonald
Compleat Vampyre - The Vampyre Shaman, Nigel Jackson
Cottage Witchcraft, Jan McDonald
Creating Form From the Mist - The Wisdom of Women in Celtic Myth and
    Culture, Lynne Sinclair-Wood
Crystal Clear - A Guide to Quartz Crystal, Jennifer Dent
Crystal Doorways, Simon & Sue Lilly
Crossing the Borderlines - Guising, Masking & Ritual Animal Disguise, Nigel Pennick
Dragons of the West, Nigel Pennick
Dreamtime by Linda Louisa Dell
Earth Dance - A Year of Pagan Rituals, Jan Brodie

Earth Harmony - Places of Power, Holiness & Healing, Nigel Pennick
Earth Magic, Margaret McArthur
Egyptian Animals - Guardians & Gateways of the Gods, Akkadia Ford
Eildon Tree (The) Romany Language & Lore, Michael Hoadley
Enchanted Forest - The Magical Lore of Trees, Yvonne Aburrow
Everything You Always Wanted To Know About Your Body, But So Far Nobody's Been Able To Tell You, Chris Thomas & D Baker
Experiencing the Green Man, Rob Hardy & Teresa Moorey
Fairies and Nature Spirits, Teresa Moorey
Fairies in the Irish Tradition, Molly Gowen
Familiars - Animal Powers of Britain, Anna Franklin
Flower Wisdom, Katherine Kear
Fool's First Steps, (The) Chris Thomas
Forest Paths - Tree Divination, Brian Harrison, Ill. S. Rouse
From Past to Future Life, Dr Roger Webber
From Stagecraft To Witchcraft, Patricia Crowther
God Year, The, Nigel Pennick & Helen Field
Goddess on the Cross, Dr George Young
Goddess Year, The, Nigel Pennick & Helen Field
Goddesses, Guardians & Groves, Jack Gale
Handbook For Pagan Healers, Liz Joan
Handbook of Fairies, Ronan Coghlan
Healing Book, The, Chris Thomas and Diane Baker
Healing Homes, Jennifer Dent
Healing Stones, Sue Philips
Heathen Paths - Viking and Anglo Saxon Beliefs by Pete Jennings
Herb Craft - Shamanic & Ritual Use of Herbs, Lavender & Franklin
In Search of Herne the Hunter, Eric Fitch
In Search of the Green Man, Peter Hill
Inner Celtia, Alan Richardson & David Annwn
Inner Mysteries of the Goths, Nigel Pennick
In Search of Pagan Gods, Teresa Moorey
Isis - African Queen, Akkadia Ford
Journey Home, The, Chris Thomas
Kecks, Keddles & Kesh - Celtic Lang & The Cog Almanac, Bayley
Language of the Psycards, Berenice
Legend of Robin Hood, The, Richard Rutherford-Moore
Lid Off the Cauldron, Patricia Crowther
Light From the Shadows - Modern Traditional Witchcraft, Gwyn
Lore of the Sacred Horse, Marion Davies
Lost Lands & Sunken Cities (2nd ed.), Nigel Pennick
Lyblác, Anglo Saxon Witchcraft by Wulfeage
The Magic and Mystery of Trees, Teresa Moorey
Magic For the Next 1,000 Years, Jack Gale
Magic of Herbs - A Complete Home Herbal, Rhiannon Ryall
Magical Guardians - Exploring the Spirit and Nature of Trees, Philip Heselton

Magical History of the Horse, Janet Farrar & Virginia Russell
Magical Lore of Animals, Yvonne Aburrow
Magical Lore of Cats, Marion Davies
Magical Lore of Herbs, Marion Davies
The Magical Properties of Plants - and How to Find Them by Tylluan Penry
Magick Without Peers, Ariadne Rainbird & David Rankine
Masks of Misrule - Horned God & His Cult in Europe, Nigel Jackson
Mind Massage - 60 Creative Visualisations, Marlene Maundrill
Mirrors of Magic - Evoking the Spirit of the Dewponds, P Heselton
The Moon and You, Teresa Moorey
Moon Mysteries, Jan Brodie
Mysteries of the Runes, Michael Howard
Mystic Life of Animals, Ann Walker
New Celtic Oracle The, Nigel Pennick & Nigel Jackson
Pagan Feasts - Seasonal Food for the 8 Festivals, Franklin & Phillips
Paganism For Teens, Jess Wynne
Patchwork of Magic - Living in a Pagan World, Julia Day
Pathworking - A Practical Book of Guided Meditations, Pete Jennings
Personal Power, Anna Franklin
Pickingill Papers - The Origins of Gardnerian Wicca, Bill Liddell
Pillars of Tubal Cain, Nigel Jackson
Planet Earth - The Universe's Experiment, Chris Thomas
Practical Divining, Richard Foord
Practical Meditation, Steve Hounsome
Psychic Self Defence - Real Solutions, Jan Brodie
Real Fairies, David Tame
Reality - How It Works & Why It Mostly Doesn't, Rik Dent
Romany Tapestry, Michael Houghton
Runic Astrology, Nigel Pennick
Sacred Animals, Gordon MacLellan
Sacred Celtic Animals, Marion Davies, Ill. Simon Rouse
Sacred Dorset - On the Path of the Dragon, Peter Knight
Sacred Grove - The Mysteries of the Forest, Yvonne Aburrow
Sacred Geometry, Nigel Pennick
Sacred Ring - Pagan Origins of British Folk Festivals, M. Howard
Season of Sorcery - On Becoming a Wisewoman, Poppy Palin
Seasonal Magic - Diary of a Village Witch, Paddy Slade
Secret Places of the Goddess, Philip Heselton
Secret Signs & Sigils, Nigel Pennick
The Secrets of East Anglian Magic, Nigel Pennick
A Seeker's Guide To Past Lives, Paul Williamson
Seeking Pagan Gods, Teresa Moorey
A Seer's Guide To Crystal Divination, Gale Halloran
Self Enlightenment, Mayan O'Brien
Soul Resurgence, Poppy Palin
Spirits of the Earth series, Jaq D Hawkins

Stony Gaze, Investigating Celtic Heads John Billingsley
Subterranean Kingdom, The, revised 2nd ed, Nigel Pennick
Symbols of Ancient Gods, Rhiannon Ryall
Talking to the Earth, Gordon MacLellan
Talking With Nature, Julie Hood
Taming the Wolf - Full Moon Meditations, Steve Hounsome
Teachings of the Wisewomen, Rhiannon Ryall
Treading the Mill - Practical CraftWorking in Modern Trad Witchcraft by Nigel Pearson
Tree: Essence of Healing, Simon & Sue Lilly
Tree: Essence, Spirit & Teacher, Simon & Sue Lilly
Tree Seer, Simon & Sue Lilly
Torch and the Spear, Patrick Regan
Understanding Chaos Magic, Jaq D Hawkins
Understanding Second Sight, Dilys Gater
Understanding Spirit Guides, Dilys Gater
Understanding Star Children, Dilys Gater
The Urban Shaman, Dilys Gater
Walking the Tides - Seasonal Rhythms and Trad Lore in Natural Craft by Nigel Pearson
Water Witches, Tony Steele
Way of the Magus, Michael Howard
Weaving a Web of Magic, Rhiannon Ryall
West Country Wicca, Rhiannon Ryall
What's Your Poison? vol 1, Tina Tarrant
Wheel of the Year, Teresa Moorey & Jane Brideson
Wildwitch - The Craft of the Natural Psychic, Poppy Palin
Wildwood King , Philip Kane
A Wisewoman's Book of Tea Leaf Reading, Pat Barki
The Witching Path, Moira Stirland
The Witch's Kitchen, Val Thomas
The Witches' Heart, Eileen Smith
Witches of Oz, Matthew & Julia Philips
Witchcraft Myth Magic Mystery and... Not Forgetting Fairies, Ralph Harvey
Wondrous Land - The Faery Faith of Ireland by Dr Kay Mullin
Working With Crystals, Shirley o'Donoghue
Working With Natural Energy, Shirley o'Donoghue
Working With the Merlin, Geoff Hughes
The Zodiac Experience, Patricia Crowther

# FREE detailed catalogue
Contact: Capall Bann Publishing, Auton Farm, Milverton, Somerset, TA4 1NE
www.capallbann.co.uk